Highlights® for Children

# Growing Up
# Learning

Highlights® for Children

# Growing Up Learning

## The Key to Your Child's Potential

**Walter B. Barbe, Ph.D.**
Editor-in-Chief, *Highlights for Children*

Foreword by Alan E. Kohrt, M.D., F.A.A.P.

ACROPOLIS BOOKS LTD.
WASHINGTON, D.C.

**ACROPOLIS BOOKS, Ltd.**
Colortone Building, 2400 17th Street, N.W.
Washington, D.C. 20009

**Printed in the United States of America by**
COLORTONE PRESS
Creative Graphics, Inc.
Washington, D.C. 20009

**Attention: Schools and Corporations**
ACROPOLIS books are available at quantity discounts with bulk purchase for educational, business, or sales promotional use. For further information, please write to: SPECIAL SALES DEPARTMENT, ACROPOLIS BOOKS, LTD., 2400 17th ST., N.W., WASHINGTON, D.C. 20009.

**Are there Acropolis Books you want but cannot find in your local stores?**
You can get any Acropolis book title in print. Simply send title and retail price, plus 50 cents for postage and handling costs for each book desired. District of Columbia residents, add applicable sales tax. Enclose check or money order only (no cash, please) to: ACROPOLIS BOOKS, LTD., 2400 17th ST., N.W., WASHINGTON, D.C. 20009.

**Photo Credits**
Ingbert Grüttner: Cover, pp. 17, 24, 57, 61, 65, 67, 70, 89, 96, 103, 105, 106, 108, 164, 180, 181, 182, 184, 186; Charles H. Bertram: pp. 14, 22, 72, 74, 90, 116, 189; Wayne County Historical Society: p. 19; Molly Rodgers: pp. 55, 86, 104, 110, 112, 114, 118, 120, 132, 133, 134; Jim Condon: pp. 28, 35, 198; Lori Klauber: p. 29; Marcia Ann Holquist: p. 58; R. Hurst: p. 75; Ellen Uding: p. 84; other photos by Herb Press and Gene Gisson, courtesy of Highlights for Children, Inc.

A grateful acknowledgement to INSTRUCTOR magazine for material on pages 180-183, which earlier appeared in the article "Modality" by Walter B. Barbe, Ph.D., and Michael Milone, Jr., Ph.D., in the January 1980 issue of INSTRUCTOR. Also to ACROPOLIS BOOKS for activities on pages 141-142 taken from *Listening Games for Elementary Grades* by Margaret John Maxwell (Acropolis Books, 1981).

**Library of Congress Cataloging in Publication Data**
Barbe, Walter B.
  Growing Up Learning
    Written in cooperation with the children's magazine,
Highlights for Children
    Includes index.
    1. Children - Books and Reading
ISBN 0-87491-790-5(pbk)

# Contents

Foreword   9

Introduction   11

Part I An Introduction to Learning Strengths and How to
    Identify Them

1  **Learning Strengths**   13

How You Learn Best . . . Avoiding
Weaknesses . . . The Definition of
Learning . . . The Changing Role of
Education . . . How Modality Based
Education Has Evolved . . . How to Identify
Learning Strengths

2  **Identifying Your Own Learning Strength**   27

Barbe Modality Checklist (Parents) . . .
Interpreting the Results . . . What Learning
Strengths Can Mean at Home . . . Family
Relationships

3  **Identifying Your Child's Learning Strength**   39

Barbe Modality Checklist (Ages 0-4), (Ages
5-8), (Ages 9 and above) . . . Interpreting the
Results . . . The Differences among Visual,
Auditory, and Kinesthetic Children . . . Toys
and Activities for Each Learner

## Part II Your Child's Learning Strength

### 4  Your Kinesthetic Child                                    51

Learning by Doing . . . What You Can Do to
Help at Home . . . Discipline . . . Rewards . . .
At School . . . The Point of Intervention . . .
Reading . . . Handwriting . . . Arithmetic . . .
Spelling . . . Lifetime Study Habits

### 5  Your Auditory Child                                       69

Learning by Listening . . . What You Can Do
to Help at Home . . . Discipline . . .
Rewards . . . At School . . . The Point of
Intervention . . . Reading . . . Handwriting
. . . Arithmetic . . . Spelling . . . Lifetime
Study Habits

### 6  Your Visual Child                                         83

Learning by Seeing . . . What You Can Do to
Help at Home . . . Discipline . . .
Rewards . . . At School . . . The Point of
Intervention . . . Reading . . . Handwriting
. . . Arithmetic . . . Spelling . . . Lifetime
Study Habits

### 7  Your Mixed Modality Child                                 97

Mixed Modalities . . . The Child with a
Mixed Modality Strength . . . The
Visual/Auditory Learner . . . The Auditory/
Kinesthetic Learner . . . The
Visual/Kinesthetic Learner . . . The
Visual/Auditory/Kinesthetic
Learner . . . How You Can Help

## Part III Spending Time with Your Child

**8   Playing with Your Child**                    109

Games . . . Party Ideas with Games and
Crafts . . . Toys

**9   Developing Basic Skills**                    135

Reading Readiness . . . Puzzles, Headwork,
and Creative Thinking . . . Tricks and
Teasers . . . Crafts . . . Books For Your Child

## Part IV Your Child's Success

**10   Your Child in School**                    179

Modality-Based Instruction . . . Teachers'
Modality Strengths . . . A Visit to a
Classroom . . . Modality-Based Instructional
Materials . . . When You Visit the
School . . . What to Do When Your Child
Needs Help

**11   Helping Your Child Capitalize on Learning
Strengths**                    193

Learning to Learn . . . Which is the Most
Effective Learning Modality? . . . Children
Doing Their Best

**Selected Readings**                    201


**Index**                    203

# Foreword

**A**s a pediatrician, a physician, I try to help parents keep their children healthy—to prevent illness, pain, and suffering. Today we are able to focus on the whole child, the emotional and mental as well as the physical well being. Fortunately, most of our children are free from the physical diseases of the past centuries. However, our society has a new array of problems with new symptoms. Among the most common "new problems" are learning disabilities, school failures, and the emotional damage that follows. These are the most complex, most frustrating difficulties that children, parents, educators, and physicians face today. Parents and teachers can use this book not only to prevent school failure, but also to help children realize their full potential.

This book provides you as parents with tools to understand how your child learns. In easy-to-understand terms it can help you help your child to learn. You will be able to recognize your child's learning style, your child's own unique strengths and weaknesses. Once you know his or her learning modality you will be able to help your child at home and help his teachers teach him at school. No matter what your child's ability or disability, this book can help both you and your child.

Dr. Barbe's concept of using visual, auditory, and kinesthetic learning styles will be beneficial because of what you can do with it and what you can *avoid* doing. By teaching the child in ways he can understand, you will not be forcing him to learn through a weakness. When we try to teach a child through a weak modality he becomes frustrated, angry, and defeated.

Over time, this leads to the child who fails, who gives up and eventually loses all self-esteem, all self-confidence.

Dr. Barbe's theories of learning styles or modalities have been developed after many years of practical experience, scientific research, and discussion. As I have learned in my own practice, his theories of modality strengths can be used to unlock the potential of all children. Children who are learning disabled, who are gifted, who are having trouble in school can be reached if we know the right way. Over the past few years, in the educational courses I have taken on learning disabilities and school problems and in my reading, the concepts of visual and auditory perception, and visual and auditory memory have been presented time after time. Dr. Barbe has added to this an area we all knew was there, but never understood as well as he did; that is, the kinesthetic modality. By knowing this triad of visual, auditory, and kinesthetic learners, we gain a much better understanding of how our children react in an educational experience. The importance of understanding the kinesthetic learner cannot be understated. Dr. Barbe's insights into this type of learner can help us better understand some of the children who are labeled "hyperactive" but who are not— They are kinesthetic learners who need a different style of teaching, not unnecessary medications.

After hearing about learning strengths from Dr. Barbe, several of our friends wanted to be tested along with their children. Through the test and general observation each of us recognized our learning strength. As we were discussing these, one woman (now a grandmother whose own children had had school difficulties) said, "It is not important what percentage of each modality we are. What *is* important is that we recognize that children are different in how they learn. We must be sure we use the appropriate method for each child."

You have a wonderful experience ahead of you—with this book you can look inside yourself and inside your child and begin to understand how your minds work. It is an exciting and challenging task, but one that will benefit you and especially your child for the rest of your lives.

—Alan E. Kohrt, M.D., F.A.A.P.

## Introduction

# The Key to Your Child's Potential

**W**e all want our children to reach their full potential, to be all that they can be. The purpose of this book is to help you, as a parent, discover the key to that potential by understanding *how* your child learns. It is as important to know *how* your child learns as *what* he or she is learning. If you can help your child "learn to learn," you will be unlocking the door to a world of almost limitless possibilities.

We each learn in our own special way. How we learn is determined by what we are born with and by our experiences in life. Many factors, therefore, can influence the way we learn best. Perception is the way we gain meaning from sensations. While we perceive through all of our senses, in most learning situations the most relevant are sight, hearing, and kinesthesia (touch and movement).

My research and that of many other educational psychologists indicate that each of us relies predominantly on one of these three, our strongest, when we are mastering a new skill or concept. We call this our *learning strength* or *modality strength*. As you have matured, you may have "learned to learn" through one or more of your other modalities; but when some new challenge comes your way, you will still depend on your strongest modality—either visual, auditory, or kinesthetic.

As an adult you may already know which of these is your strength, or at least have a clue. This book will help you identify your child's learning strength, then give you ideas for helping him capitalize on his strength, rather than his weaknesses, to master new skills and concepts all his life. If he knows how he learns best, he can tackle life with pride and confidence, instead of frustration.

It stands to reason that if you teach a child the way he learns most easily, he will learn better. This is the essence of modality-based education.

As parents and teachers we naturally teach children the way we ourselves learn best. Unfortunately, this is the best method only when our way is also the child's best way. For instance, if we learn best through verbal instructions, we think everyone else does. And if our children don't understand what we are telling them right away, we repeat it over and over again. "I've told you a thousand times," we insist. But the fault is not with the child. It is with us. We aren't "telling" them so that they can "hear" us.

Modality-based education is not new. But until now it has been used almost exclusively to teach children with learning problems in academic settings.

In previous books I have demonstrated for teachers how to teach to children's strengths, instead of to their weaknesses. Now I hope to show you, as parents, how to do the same thing, in the home setting. You are your children's own first and best teacher. It is your love and understanding that can help them grow up learning.

—Walter B. Barbe, Ph.D.

No book is written without the assistance of family, colleagues and friends. Molly Rodgers has worked with me on modalities for several years and Kathleen Hughes helped in bringing these ideas together. The staff of *Highlights for Children* and *The Newsletter of Parenting* contributed their skills. Without their help and the help of parents around the country, *Growing Up Learning* would not have been.

—W.B.B.

*Chapter 1*

# Learning Strengths

Learning begins at home, in your arms. So it is only fitting that this book share with you, the parent, important knowledge about learning that has been gained through many years of research and experience in teaching children. So far most of our findings have been used in academic settings. But since so much learning takes place in your own home, it is vital that you understand how your child learns.

Children learn by seeing, hearing, moving and touching. For each child, one of these channels—visual, auditory, or kinesthetic—is the one through which he or she learns best. Knowing your child's learning strength and using that knowledge will make learning and living together easier. It will decrease the frustration and increase the self-confidence your child will experience. It can help your child increase his or her academic achievement, improve attitudes toward school, and even reduce discipline problems.

## How You Learn Best

Think back to a time when you were struggling to learn something new. Picture yourself sitting at your desk in elementary school, studying for a spelling test. Did you rely on looking at the spelling list on the board or your paper, and forming a visual picture of each word? Could you tell when a word was misspelled simply by looking at it or writing it out to see if it looked right? Or, did you say the letters and sounds of the word over and over to yourself? Did you have to spell a word out loud to tell if it was spelled correctly? Did you do better in

**Understanding how your child learns makes learning and living together easier for the whole family.**

spelling bees than in written spelling tests? Or, can you remember fidgeting and squirming, having to write the word over and over again until you learned it?

Your answers to these questions are clues to your own learning strength. If you learned by looking at each word, taking a "photograph" of it in your mind, and if you can tell that a word is misspelled simply by looking at it, you are most likely a *visual* learner. You learn best by seeing or looking.

If you sound words out to spell them, you are an *auditory* learner. You learn to spell words by hearing others spell them, and by saying the letters aloud yourself. You learn best through verbal instructions and talking problems out.

If you need to write a word, to "feel" whether or not it is misspelled, you are a *kinesthetic* learner. You learn most efficiently by being directly involved with a new skill, by doing it, rather than seeing it or hearing about it.

Here is another example. Do you remember faces, but forget names? Do you have to write things down and take notes? Do you think in pictures? Then you are a *visual* learner.

Or, do you remember names, but forget faces? Do you hum a lot and talk to yourself when you are doing a project? Then you are an *auditory* learner.

Or, do you remember best what you have physically participated in? Do you say, "Let me try," knowing that until you actually "do" it yourself you are not really going to learn? When you remember, is the image accompanied by movement? Do you actively try out different solutions to problems? Then you are a *kinesthetic* learner.

## Avoiding Weaknesses

As an adult, you have most likely learned through experience to transfer information from one channel to another, and to apply your learning strength in areas that are difficult. One of the sure signs of being an adult is knowing just what you are weak in. No one will ever catch us doing something willingly, especially in front of others, that we know we don't do well.

Our children are not so lucky. In many academic settings, they are tested and confronted with their failures. They are given endless hours of practice, not in their areas of strength, but in their areas of weakness. Eventually this can destroy their self-confidence and their willingness to learn. At home, too, we expect our children to do things the way we do. If our learning strength is different from theirs, we may not be reinforcing their strengths.

Directing children to their most efficient learning channel will help them be successful learners and overcome their deficiencies. They will learn to learn and enjoy doing it.

## The Definition of Learning

True learning is the ability to apply a skill or fact to real life. But, as we have said, each person has a different way of learning. This book will help you answer these questions:

How do you learn best?

How does your spouse learn best?

How does your child learn best?

Is the way you learn the same way your children learn?

Do all of your children learn the same way?

Does your spouse understand your child's learning strength?

Does your child's teacher understand your child's learning strength?

What can you do to help?

Many factors influence your child's learning. The most important of these is *perception:* how he gains meaning from the environment. Perception begins with our five senses: hearing, seeing, tasting, smelling, and feeling. The term "modality" in educational terms refers particularly to *vision, audition,* and *kinesthesia.* The *visual modality* includes both sight and mental imagery. The *auditory modality* refers to hearing and speaking. And the *kinesthetic modality* means large and small muscle movements, as well as touching with the fingers. Some authors and researchers separate the kinesthetic abilities and treat them individually. But for practical purposes, discussing large muscle, small muscle, and tactile abilities together reflects the behavior of children better than treating each separately.

While everyone uses all three modalities for learning, most of us rely on one or two in times of intense concentration, great need, or stress. The modality or sensory channel we depend on is called our *learning strength* or *dominant modality.* It may change over time as we learn to adjust to different learning situations, but most people have a well-established channel to learning, one that is most efficient for receiving and retaining information.

In addition to a dominant modality, many people have a secondary modality upon which they can rely when the situation demands it. A secondary modality is not so efficient as the dominant one, but it can complement or enhance it. If a child needs additional explanation or practice on a skill, she can use

**Children enjoy learning when they use their strengths—seeing, hearing, moving, and touching.**

the secondary modality for support. The third modality, after the dominant and secondary, is viewed as the area of weakness. When information is presented in this modality, the individual will have greatest difficulty understanding and retaining the information.

Mixed modalities occur when no single modality is clearly dominant. Since the proportion of persons with mixed modalities is larger among adults than children, it is likely that maturity and the opportunity to practice in all three modalities over the years are the principal reasons that mixed modalities occur. Children with mixed modality strengths generally have an easier time in the classroom since they are able to process information in two or three modalities with equal efficiency.

We are born with certain characteristics that contribute to our later learning strengths. The experiences we encounter in early life, such as nutrition, stimulation, and interactions with other children and adults, may also influence which learning channels will be strongest. By the time we reach adulthood, both genetics and experience have influenced the way we learn best.

## The Changing Role of Education

Never before has it been so important for our children to be successful learners, whether they continue through college, professional school, technical training, or vocational school. Our complex world presents an ever-increasing store of information to be learned, and our children are being pressured in their earliest years to begin reading, writing, and arithmetic. In turn, our schools are pressured to teach more, teach better. Much publicity has been given to what is wrong with our schools and why our children are not learning. People ask what happened to the good old days when everyone learned. But, as Will Rogers quipped, "The schools ain't the same, and they never was." And I would add, "Thank goodness!"

In the good old days people learned in the rigid way offered or they did not stay in school. If a child did not fit the norm he was put aside. However, the lack of formal education did not necessarily mean failure either. Many people were great successes in life with only a few years of schooling. They were

**At the turn of the century, the rigid form of education did not allow for individual differences.**

the ones who found their strengths and could continue learning independently. Those who stayed in school were the ones who fit the mold and took what was given. No longer can our society afford to pay the price of a too rigid education. Democracy depends on the full development of all its citizens. And we as parents know that education is the key to a better life for our children. We want them to be aware of their strengths, to be self-confident. We are willing to devote the time to help them toward this goal. Schools and teachers are devoted to the same cause.

We hear more about the problems in school because the schools are more willing to face the problems and do something about them. Before remedial education, many children just did not learn. Today, the schools are doing more to teach each child as well as he or she can learn. The emphasis for both teachers and parents must be on the learning process, not just how much is learned.

School systems are being judged by their pupils' achievement on standardized tests. In many areas parents buy or rent houses on the basis of the local school system's performance, as judged by these scores. Pressures to begin learning have contributed significantly to preschool enrollments. But the wisdom of such pressure is certainly debatable. We cannot teach our children all that they will need to know. The crux of the matter is not how early to start learning to learn more, but simply how to learn, how to enjoy learning so that the world is open to our children.

I recently heard a story about a young boy who was talking to his father after school. The boy had been in first grade for several weeks, and his parents were very concerned with what his class was doing in reading. He and his father had been going over one of his books when he looked up and asked, "How many years will I be in school?" Adding in college, his father replied, "Sixteen." The boy popped up, looking a little relieved, and said, "Well, I have *plenty* of time to learn to read!"

It turns out this boy is quite kinesthetic, and at the time, other things were more interesting to him than sitting at a desk learning to read. This same boy is now in the third grade and doing well. He excels in all sorts of handwork, especially wood-carving. He can carve names, dates, almost anything. He learned his letters by drawing them in the sandbox. He does not spend a long time reading, but whenever there is something he wants to *do,* or something he wants to know more about, he will find a book to help him learn. Making this boy learn to read before he was ready might have resulted in his disliking it altogether. Using reading to enrich his active interests can only help him appreciate reading more. As long as he knows that books are a resource for finding knowledge, this boy can take off in any direction he chooses. In the competition to get ahead and stay ahead, it is the child who understands how he learns and has confidence in his strength who has unlimited potential.

## How Modality-Based Education Has Evolved

Our tradition of teaching writing by auditory, visual, and kinesthetic methods goes back through the European languages, including Latin, to the ancient Greeks and earlier peoples of the Mediterranean. In the ninth century B.C. the Greeks developed the alphabet with consonants and vowels which became the basis for their writing and source of the alphabet as we know it. It was an adaptation of an existing script, but it was a brilliant improvement destined to have lasting influence.

Long before any alphabet evolved, even before pictographs and ideographs of such peoples as the Egyptians and the Chinese, information was transmitted by word of mouth. Understandably, when writing was developed, people continued to use auditory methods to teach children to read. Their phonetic method of teaching children to read by sounding out the words is part of our universal heritage.

So also are kinesthetic methods. The ancient Greeks taught writing to their children by having them trace the letters with a stylus or by actually guiding their hands through the motions of shaping each letter.

The Incas, who never invented true writing, developed a unique auditory-kinesthetic method for recording narratives and numbers. They had knotted strings, called *quipus,* which consisted of a main cord from which hung smaller strings with groups of knots tied at intervals. The quipu keeper memorized the meaning of each knot—historical events, religious cere-monies—and repeated it whenever a government official needed a report. New quipu keepers were taught auditorily what each knot meant. Some quipus were used to tabulate numbers and sums, with different colors of knotted strings to represent different categories of items.

We now know that the Romans used a visual-auditory method of teaching. Students were required to say words and letters aloud while looking at a printed copy of those same words and letters. This method was the basis of English and American textbooks well into the eighteenth century.

All through history, educators have preferred visual and auditory methods to kinesthetic methods. This prejudice may have begun with the Greeks; but even today many teachers believe that visual and auditory tasks are best for all children. True, they work for visual and auditory learners, but not as well for kinesthetic children.

The famous educator, Maria Montessori, introduced modality-based education in this century. She was trained as a doctor; but soon after completing her medical degree, she became concerned with the plight of retarded, emotionally disturbed, and other disadvantaged children in her native Rome.

**Maria Montessori's teaching methods based on sensory stimulation, are used successfully today.**

These children had been thought to be almost uneducable.

Montessori did not agree. She discovered that when children's senses are stimulated, they gain perceptual skills. Once these skills have been mastered, the transition from purely sensory materials, such as shapes and blocks, to three-dimensional representations of letters can be made. When children can recognize letters, they can learn to write, and then to read. Her program involves first educating the senses, then educating the intellect. Montessori and her followers achieved greater success with learning-disabled children than any previous educators. Her methods are used successfully today with slow learners, average, and gifted children.

The decades from 1930 to 1970 brought an increasing recognition of the essential role of the modalities, and of the varying modality strengths within each child which should be identified. Most educators continued to feel that vision was the most important receptive mode; however, they did acknowledge the importance of motor activities as a basis for learning. The focus was still on developing children's weaknesses rather than using strengths to help learning.

Through the 1960s educators such as Marianne Frostig were working on material to assess visual and auditory perception and to train deficient areas. This approach received widespread support at the time because success—as measured by a child's improvement on a particular task—was achieved. However, later research pointed out that there was little transfer of skills into acquiring or retaining new knowledge. When a child was taught outside her modality strength, she learned the task but could not apply it. When faced with a related task at another time, the child would revert to her dominant modality and had to relearn the task.

When modality-based education was first brought into the general classroom it was interpreted as "multi-sensory instruction," meaning using more than one way to teach a particular subject. This was not true modality-based instruction, and it met with mixed success because of weaknesses in its approach. Multi-sensory instruction took two forms. One was to direct a barrage of multi-sensory material toward the class in the hope that each student's learning strength would be hit by at least part of the lesson. For some students such presentations, with information presented in three modalities at once, were not only distracting, but actually inhibited learning.

The other form of multi-sensory instruction was to teach a lesson through one modality, repeat the same lesson through another modality, and finally present it again through the remaining modality. The problem was that most of the class was ignored for two-thirds of the lesson. Some students would tune out irrelevant aspects while they waited for the appropriate material. Others would attend to all three styles of presentation and become confused by the different forms one lesson could take.

The other problem with multi-sensory instruction was that it overlooked teachers' modality strengths. What was intended to be multi-sensory would naturally shift to favor a teacher's own dominant modality without the teacher recognizing the shift. As we now understand modality-based education, it is most successful when the teacher recognizes his own modality strength and the strengths of his students. The teacher presents material the way in which he is most comfortable, accommodating students' modality strengths when possible. At the point one or more students do not grasp the material as initially presented the teacher alters lesson strategies to involve students' learning strengths.

## How to Identify Learning Strengths

Before modality-based instruction can begin, teachers must be able to assess modality strengths. There are a number of assessment instruments available to teachers but many teachers will use such tools only to verify their observations or to clarify conflicting behaviors. For most teachers, experience with children quickly sensitizes them to modality behaviors, and it is a matter of common sense as to what works with a particular child. I have observed children during testing and identified modality strengths even before scores have been calculated. When testing becomes difficult, visual children are most likely to look off at a blank wall or up at the ceiling, trying to "see" the answer they are searching for. Auditory children will talk to themselves, repeating material until it sounds right. Kinesthetic children will fidget, squirm in their chairs, and play with their hands, trying to get a "feel" for the answer. For your purposes as a parent, the modality checklists in Chapters 2 and 3 offer a guide to help you identify, first of all, how you learn, and then how your child learns. The most frequent learning strengths are visual and a combination or mixed modality strengths. About 30 percent of the population is visual, and 30 percent is

**Most teachers quickly become sensitive to their students' modality behaviors.**

*Growing Up Learning*

mixed. Auditory learners account for approximately 25 percent of the population; and the rest, about 15 percent, are kinesthetic.

Before you begin the individual modality checklists, you need to become sensitive to the characteristics of each of the three learning modalities. The chart that follows lists behaviors indicative of visual, auditory, and kinesthetic learners. This chart is not meant to set forth hard and fast rules. Behaviors listed do not always indicate one specific modality strength. You need to take care to avoid labeling either yourself or your child on the basis of one or two isolated behaviors. Every individual makes use of all the modalities (unless there is a physical disability). Therefore, at various times a person may behave in a way that might indicate any one of the three modalities. The chart and the checklists can help you understand what to look for over a period of time.

Once you are familiar with modality-related behaviors, you can use the checklists to confirm your observations about yourself and your child. The checklists in Chapter 3 are divided into age groups: zero to four years old, five to eight, and nine and above. Learning strengths can be observed even in infants.

## Table 1.  Modality Characteristics You Can Observe

| | Visual | Auditory | Kinesthetic |
|---|---|---|---|
| Learning Style | Learns by seeing; watching demonstrations | Learns through verbal instructions from others or self | Learns by doing; direct involvement |
| Reading | Likes description; sometimes stops reading to stare into space and imagine scene; | Enjoys dialogue, plays; avoids lengthy description, unaware of illustrations; moves lips or subvocalizes | Prefers stories where action occurs early; fidgets when reading, handles books; not an avid reader |
| Spelling | Recognizes words by sight; relies on configuration of words | Uses a phonics approach; has auditory word attack skills | Often is a poor speller; writes words to determine if they "feel" right |
| Handwriting | Tends to be good, particularly when young; appearance is important | Has more difficulty learning in initial stages; tends to write lightly; says strokes when writing | Good initially, deteriorates when space becomes smaller; pushes harder on pencil |
| Memory | Remembers faces, forgets names; writes things down, takes notes | Remembers names, forgets faces; remembers by auditory repetition | Remembers best what was done, not what was seen or talked about |

# Table 1.   (continued)

| | Visual | Auditory | Kinesthetic |
|---|---|---|---|
| Imagery | Vivid imagination; thinks in pictures, visualizes in detail | Subvocalizes, thinks in sounds; details less important | Imagery not important; images that do occur are accompanied by movement |
| Distractibility | Generally unaware of sounds; distracted by visual disorder or movement | Easily distracted by sounds | Not attentive to visual, auditory presentation so seems distractible |
| Problem Solving | Deliberate; plans in advance; organizes thoughts by writing them; lists problems | Talks problems out, tries solutions verbally, subvocally; | Attacks problems physically; impulsive; selects solution with greatest activity |
| Response to Periods of Inactivity | Stares; doodles; finds something to watch | Hums; talks to self or to others | Fidgets; finds reasons to move; holds up hand |
| Response to New Situations | Looks around; examines structure | Talks about situation, pros and cons, what to do | Tries things out; touches, feels; manipulates |
| Emotionality | Somewhat repressed; stares when angry; cries easily, beams when happy; facial expression is a good index of emotion | Shouts with joy or anger; blows up verbally but soon calms down; expresses emotion through changes in tone, volume, pitch | Jumps for joy; hugs, tugs, and pulls when happy; stamps, pounds when angry, stomps off; general body tone is a good index of emotion |
| Communication | Quiet; does not talk at length; impatient when extensive listening is required; may use words clumsily; uses words such as *see, look*, etc. | Enjoys listening but cannot wait to talk; descriptions are long but repetitive; likes hearing self, others; uses words such as *listen, hear*, etc. | Gestures when speaking, stands close; does not listen well; uses words such as *get, take*, etc. |
| General Appearance | Neat, meticulous, likes order; may choose not to vary appearance | Matching clothes not so important, can explain choices of clothes | Neat but soon becomes wrinkled through activity |
| Response to the Arts | Prefers the visual arts; tends not to voice appreciation of art of any kind, but can be deeply affected by visual displays; focuses on details and components rather than the work as a whole | Favors music; finds less appeal in visual art but is readily able to discuss it; misses significant detail, but appreciates the work as a whole; is able to develop verbal association for all art forms | Responds to music by physical movement; prefers sculpture; touches statues and paintings; at exhibits stops only at those in which he or she can become physically involved; comments very little on any art form |

# Chapter 2

# Identifying Your Own Learning Strength

How can a person determine what his or her dominant modality or learning style really is? You need to become sensitive to the concept, understand what it means, and then sharpen your observational ability. As you become more aware of your own behavior and that of others, you will begin to notice the signs of learning strengths. For example, the language a person uses is one easily observable clue. Visual people say such things as "Do you see what I mean? and "Look at me when I talk to you." Auditory people say "Listen to me" and "Did you hear me?" Kinesthetic people do not use excessive language, and tend to say a short phrase such as "Get it?" or to make no comment.

An observation I have made during my years of lecturing to groups of parents, teachers, and students is that visual people tend to sit in the front row, right up where they can see best. The auditory people sit in the middle, so they can concentrate on listening to what I have to say, without the visual distractions of my walking around the stage. And, the kinesthetic people sit right near the door, so if they don't like what they are hearing or think I've been talking too long, they can make a quick escape.

To begin with, we need some kind of a guide. A checklist is just that—a guide that helps us sharpen our observational skills. The checklists included in this book are intended only as a beginning guide, and the results you get the first time you use them may vary from the results you get when you think about your responses and answer the questions at a later time. You may also want to discuss some of the items with people who know you. They may see that you do certain things differently from the way you marked the checklist.

A major difficulty with a checklist is that we tend to mark the items as we wish we were, rather than as we actually are. Or we may mark it the way someone has convinced us is the so-called "correct" way. It is easy for us to fool even ourselves. But as time passes, and we have an opportunity to think about the items and observe others as well as ourselves, we usually become better observers. Then we are better at answering the items and our results have more meaning.

Sometimes, when a person has one modality that is particularly strong, it may be difficult for him or her to perceive

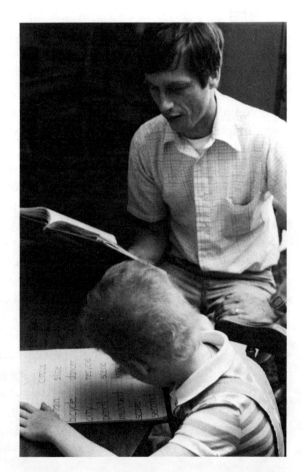

**Observing your child as he works will give you clues to his learning strength.**

**Be alert to the times when learning can better take place through your child's learning strength.**

beyond that mode. Such people tend to insist that they use all three, almost to the point of being unable to accept that there is a difference in the way people do things. There is so clearly a "right" way to such individuals that it is easy for them to interpret their behavior as using all three, when in reality they are only using one mode. Such individuals will benefit from asking another person to check over their responses and see if they agree. In such a case it is best to answer all ten items and then compare responses. Reviewing the checklist item by item may only invite argument from someone with a strong, single dominant modality.

The goal is not just completing the checklist and determining a "score." The goal is to become sensitive to the existence of modality strengths, and to be alert to the times when learning can better take place through your or your child's dominant mode.

# Barbe Modality Checklist (Parents)

## A Key to Your Own Learning Strength

Listed below are incomplete sentences, each followed by three ways of completing it. Distribute 10 points among the three phrases. Divide the 10 points according to how strongly each phrase describes you. The phrase that describes you best would get more points than the phrase that least describes you. For instance, if you believe each phrase describes you equally well, mark a 3 in two blanks and a 4 in the one which you favor even slightly more. If you are completely described by one of the phrases, mark a 10 by it and a 0 by the other two. Remember, you *must* use a total of ten points for each statement.

A. My emotions can often be interpreted from my:

— facial expressions.

— voice quality.

— general body tone.

B. I keep up with current events by:

— reading the newspaper thoroughly when I have time.

— listening to the radio or watching the television news.

— reading the headlines or spending a few minutes watching television news.

C. If I have business to conduct I prefer to:

— write letters, since I then have a record.

— telephone, since it saves time.

— converse while doing something (such as holding a pencil, tapping my foot, etc.).

getting tired.

| | Visual | Auditory | Kinesthetic |
|---|---|---|---|
| F. When dressing, I consider: | color and coordination of clothes. | nothing in particular, but I can explain why I picked which clothes. | what I will be doing and how comfortable I want to be. |
| G. At a meeting, I: | take notes, watch people's faces. | enjoy discussions in which I have an opportunity to present my point of view. | like frequent breaks. |
| H. In my spare time, I would rather: | watch television, go to a movie or the theater, read. | listen to the radio or records, attend a concert, play an instrument, talk to friends. | engage in physical activity of some kind (sports, handwork, etc.). |
| I. Under stress, I would discipline a child by: | separating the child from the group, giving a stern look. | scolding, telling the child what he or she did wrong. | holding child's arm, picking child up, other physical action. |
| J. When rewarding a child, I: | smile, give stick-ons, post child's work for others to see. | give oral praise to child. | give a hug, a pat on the back. |
| **Total** | _____ Visual | _____ Auditory | _____ Kinesthetic |

## Interpreting the Results

Add your score in each of the three columns. The total should equal 100. Each of the three scores represents the degree to which you use or depend upon that modality. A difference of plus or minus 5 points is not significant. It means you are about equal in those two or even three modalities. Some people have a single learning strength or modality; others have a mixed dominance, with the ability to use two modalities effectively (visual-auditory, visual-kinesthetic, auditory-kinesthetic). You may have discovered that you are comfortable in all three: you can process information no matter how it is presented.

Actually, all of us are able to use each of the three modalities, but in varying degrees. Experience teaches us to which degree we are comfortable using each. And, as adults, we have learned to integrate our modalities, to transfer information from one modality to another as the situation demands. But in times of stress we revert to our strongest modality (or secondary modality if necessary) and avoid our weakest if at all possible.

A woman who has been a state legislator for ten years told me recently that when she was first elected and had to attend public hearings, she liked to read the testimony of speakers as they gave it. Some of her colleagues asked her why she needed to do all that reading. They spent their time questioning speakers and listening to their responses to form opinions. She needed to see things in writing before making a judgment. After ten years and severe restrictions on her time, she is now able to do more listening and less reading, but she depended upon her visual strength, her dominant modality, to learn her job.

## What Learning Strengths Can Mean at Home

If you are a visual parent, your house is probably neatly organized, and children's artwork is displayed in at least one prominent place, along with shopping lists and notes to various family members. You have most likely decorated your child's room with the same attention to visual delights, books and toys arranged tidily on shelves, a blackboard, easel, crayons, and markers ready for quiet activity. It may annoy you when a busy child does not feel the same need to keep her room neat, when she fails to put everything back in the spaces you have so thoughtfully created for her.

If you are an auditory parent, on the other hand, your house may seem cluttered to the visually oriented. But that doesn't bother you. You know exactly where everything is, and you can concentrate with papers stacked around you, the telephone ringing, and music playing loudly. You will have provided your children with a record player or a tape deck and lots of stories and songs to play on them. You are the parent who tells your child how to do things and is annoyed when he doesn't respond immediately. But it is in your household that problems are "talked" through and listening is most important.

If you are a kinesthetic parent, you, too, are not concerned with tidiness. Your desk and kitchen counter are as much storage areas as they are work areas. The kitchen will be used for all sorts of projects from concocting a big pot of clay to making a bird house. Bikes, roller skates, and balls decorate the play area and are rarely left unused for long. Activity is the symbol of your household.

**Activity is the symbol of your household if you are a kinesthetic parent.**

In other words, you have created an environment that is comfortable for your learning strength; and you are teaching your child in the way that has always worked best for you. If your child has the same learning strength, everything is just fine. But if he does not, then there may be many times when you don't understand each other.

Eight-year-old Sam was a child who loved to take things apart to see what was inside of them. At two he had succeeded in unscrewing the cap on the fire hydrant outside of his house. He delighted in taking out all of his toys, never one at a time; but his visual mother could not teach him to put things back the way she wanted them. At the end of every afternoon of vigorous play, she would ask him to put his toys away. She even handed him the boxes to put them in. Finally, in despair, she threw all the toys in a big box, forgetting the shelves and little boxes they had come in. The next day Sam got out all of his toys, played happily, then just as happily put them all back into the great big box before running outside. He was a kinesthetic child who responded to the big box as if it were another game, but who could never remember his mother's careful instructions for putting each toy in a special place. His mother learned to provide big spaces for him and to tell him something right before she wanted him to do it. Sam liked to attack problems physically. Putting the toys back into the big box required as much movement and activity as taking them out.

## Family Relationships

Just as your modality affects the physical environment of your home, so it influences the relationships within. We communicate best in our own modality. How frequently we communicate, how long we speak or listen, what form our communication takes is different for each of us. Recognizing the different modality strengths in your family can make communication more effective.

If you are visual, you probably do not talk at length, nor do you listen for extended periods of time without looking off, staring into space, or finding some focus for your attention. When angry or bothered you do not usually come right out and speak your mind. Your family needs to learn to watch you and read your face for signals of emotion. Then someone can draw you into a discussion of what is troubling you. The most effective means for your spouse or child to remind you about something is to write notes and leave them in a spot you will be sure to notice.

If you are auditory, you are much more likely to talk to your spouse and your children about everything. You do not hesitate to tell them what is wrong, and you expect them to tell you as easily. You are willing to listen to your family; but you cannot sit silently—you need to be a part of the discussion. As long as your family makes sure they have your attention when

**If you are auditory, talking and listening are most important.**

they tell you something, they can depend on you to remember verbal messages. But if they shout something at you on the way out the door while you are on the phone or talking to someone else, the message may be lost.

If you are kinesthetic, there is a "no nonsense" approach to your communication. You get right to the point and do not listen well to others who elaborate or repeat things a lot. You like to stand close to people. You gesture and touch more frequently when talking. This may annoy or upset others who don't like physical contact or who don't know you well. Many times you may not even feel the need to communicate; you may just want to "get it done!" For members of your family who are not so kinesthetic, you should remind yourself to give them time to do things at their own pace. Children need to learn to do things themselves, especially when they are young and learning important tasks. It will seem easier and certainly faster for you to get them buttoned and zipped, to put away a floor full of toys, to prepare food and clean up after meals, but it will not help your children if you constantly step in and do things for them. For you, messages and reminders are best given as close as feasible to when you are to do things. For instance, your family can tell you what they need as you are getting ready to go to the store. Or you should actually write any notes and messages yourself as reminders. You may never look at the note again. The act of writing it down is often enough to help you remember.

It is the different combinations of modalities in a home that can seriously affect relationships. One auditory family member may feel no one else ever hears him. Two auditory learners may find themselves in never-ending debates. Two visual learners who are both reluctant to speak out may never bring problems out into the open and thus may never solve disagreements.

One young couple I know was hit by an extreme personal tragedy. They had trouble dealing with their grief. She is auditory and wanted to talk out all the emotions she felt. He is kinesthetic and had to work out his grief by involving himself in more and more activities. He was rarely at home. Each was trying to work through the grief in his or her own way, but they knew they weren't helping each other. Finally, they went for four days to a place away from home where they did things together and could talk to each other. Each learned to understand the other's way of coping.

Even having matching modalities does not guarantee success. An auditory mother told me recently that when she was trying to help her auditory child learn to ride her two-wheeler, it just didn't seem to work. They were communicating perfectly about the ways to ride. They talked about how to ride, how you are supposed to balance yourself, and so forth. They got the bike out and, talking away, the child tried to ride the bike as the mother helped balance it. But somehow when the child didn't just set off riding on her own, they both became disinterested. Abandoning the bike for the time being, they went inside and happily read a book together. Eventually, the child learned to ride on her own, but they certainly had a hard time—both mother and daughter—practicing the kinesthetic skills needed to ride a bike. This same child told me her favorite subject at school is recess. I discovered she loves recess, not because it gives her a chance to run around, but because it gives her a chance to sit under her favorite tree and read aloud!

As long as you are aware of your own, your spouse's, and your children's modality strengths, you are a long way toward

**Be aware that your child's modality may not be the same as your own.**

avoiding communication problems. Understanding how your children learn is an important step to understanding them as people. It is unrealistic to think that you must always adapt your learning style to others. Sometimes children must adjust their learning strengths, transferring information from one modality to another. But certainly when you want your child to concentrate on something you are trying to teach him, he will master it more readily if you understand how he learns. The same matching of teaching and learning styles that can work in school can make your teaching at home more effective.

*Chapter 3*

# Identifying Your Child's Learning Strength

You are ready to discover how your children learn best, now that you know how you learn best. Three checklists follow: one for infants-to-four-year-olds; one for five-to-eight-year-olds; and one for nine-year-olds and above.

The three checklists depend upon your observations of how your child responds in various situations. If you have more than one child, be sure to use a checklist for each. You may find that each of your children has a different learning strength, and their strengths may be different from yours.

Remember, the checklists are an aid in understanding your child. They are meant as one tool to help you discover how your child best receives and retains information. Use the results as a beginning, sensitize yourself to your child's signals, and guide your child to use his or her strength to master new skills and concepts. Your goal is to help your child learn to learn. Next to your love, it is one of the most important gifts you can ever give.

After identifying your child's learning strength, it may be most valuable to discuss with your child what you have learned. Once your child realizes that you recognize his strengths and weaknesses, two things will happen. One, he will be most pleased that you understand him, and this will enhance the child-parent relationship. Also, he will begin to recognize his own strengths and weaknesses and know which modality to rely on in times of stress.

# Barbe Modality Checklist (Ages 0-4)

## A Key to How Your Child Learns

Listed below are ten incomplete sentences followed by three phrases. Divide the 10 points among the three phrases. Distribute 10 points among the three ways of completing each. Distribute the 10 points according to how strongly each phrase describes your child. The phrase that describes your child best would receive more points than the phrase that least describes your child. For instance, if you believe each phrase describes your child equally well, mark a 3 in two blanks and a 4 in the one which favors your child even slightly more. If your child is completely described by one of the phrases, mark a *10* by it and *0* by the other two. Remember you *must* use a total of 10 points for each.

**A.** When playing, my child:
— likes details and colorful things, peers at objects, watches things.
— likes to babble and talk, prefers toys that make sounds.
— likes to move, jump, climb; prefers toys with moving parts.

**B.** During mealtime, my child:
— reacts to size of portion and colors of food.
— wants to talk, prolonging mealtime; is easily distracted by noises.
— is interested in food texture; when finished, continues to play with food and utensils.

**C.** When taking a bath, my child:
— wants all kinds of toys in the tub then plays with one at a time.
— talks to self and to toys, listens to water sounds, talks to parents.
— throws, splashes, kicks; likes toys that squirt; washes toys, tub, parents.

| | Visual | Auditory | Kinesthetic |
|---|---|---|---|
| child's attention are: | crayons, books, toys with parts to watch as they move or change. | recorder, radio, instruments. | toys to push, pull, balls, things to climb on or into. |
| E. When angry, my child: | — uses silent treatment, turns head. | — cries, whines, raises voice. | — kicks, bites, throws things. |
| F. I can tell when my child is happy by: | — his face. | — his voice. | — his body movements. |
| G. As part of our bedtime routine, my child: | — likes to look at books, prefers nightlight. | — likes to hear a story or song, talks about events, hums to self. | — likes to be held, rocked, walked around; holds stuffed animal or blanket.' |
| H. When playing with a doll or pet, my child: | — studies it, peers into eyes, ears. | — talks to it, for it; it becomes character in play. | — grabs it, carries it around, puts it in and out of things. |
| I. When looking for encouragement or reward, my child: | — looks for a smile; must have me see accomplishment. | — needs verbal praise. | — needs a hug, a pat on the back. |
| J. When riding in a car (long trip), my child: | — observes things outside, notices lights inside. | — likes radio on; makes noises, talks about where we are going. | — moves continuously, grabs things; resists car seat. |
| Total | ___ Visual | ___ Auditory | ___ Kinesthetic |

©1985, Walter B. Barbe

# Barbe Modality Checklist (Ages 5-8)

## A Key to How Your Child Learns

Listed below are incomplete sentences followed by three ways of completing each. Distribute 10 points among the three phrases. Divide the 10 points according to how strongly each phrase describes your child. The phrase that describes your child best would receive more points than the phrase that least describes your child. For instance, if you believe each phrase describes your child equally well, mark a 3 in two blanks and a 4 in the one which favors your child even slightly more. If your child is completely described by one of the phrases, mark a 10 by it and 0 by the other two. Remember you *must* use a total of 10 points for each.

**A.** When playing, my child:

— likes details and colorful things, peers at objects and moving things.

— likes to talk, prefers toys that make sounds.

— likes to move, climb, jump, use tools; prefers toys with moving parts.

**B.** During mealtime, my child:

— eats food that looks good first, sorts by color.

— talks instead of eating, prolonging meals.

— squirms in chair, may get up and down; often puts too much in mouth.

**C.** When reading or being read to, my child:

— is interested in pictures, wants to see pages.

— is concerned with sounds, asks questions.

— prefers turning pages, handling the book; doesn't sit for long.

**D.** When counting, my child:

— likes to see objects being counted

— counts aloud, may make
sense of s

— counts on fingers, likes

| | Visual | Auditory | Kinesthetic |
|---|---|---|---|
| **E.** When I scold my child he or she: | — looks away, cries. | — cries or whines, explains away fault. | — doesn't listen; avoids scolding by doing something. |
| **F.** In more formal learning (coloring, workbooks) my child: | — tries to stay in lines, uses many colors, wants things to fit in spaces. | — asks questions, talks during work. | — works rapidly, impatient to get to next page, does not stay in lines. |
| **G.** In group situations, my child: | — tends to be quiet, watches more than initiates. | — raises voice, talks at the same time as others. | — either is first or last in line; can't wait to get moving. |
| **H.** When angry my child: | — uses silent treatment, may become teary-eyed, will not look at me. | — shouts, whines. | — reacts physically, clenches fist or strikes out. |
| **I.** I can tell when my child is happy by: | — facial expression. | — voice quality. | — body movement. |
| **J.** When looking for encouragement or reward my child: | — looks for a smile, must have me see accomplishment. | — needs verbal praise. | — needs a hug, a pat on the back. |
| **Total** | ____ Visual | ____ Auditory | ____ Kinesthetic |

# Barbe Modality Checklist (Ages 9 and over)

## A Key to How Your Child Learns

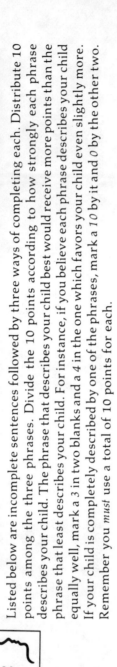

Listed below are incomplete sentences followed by three ways of completing each. Distribute 10 points among the three phrases. Divide the 10 points according to how strongly each phrase describes your child. The phrase that describes your child best would receive more points than the phrase that least describes your child. For instance, if you believe each phrase describes your child equally well, mark a 3 in two blanks and a 4 in the one which favors your child even slightly more. If your child is completely described by one of the phrases, mark a 10 by it and 0 by the other two. Remember you *must* use a total of 10 points for each.

**A.** My child's emotions can be interpreted by:
— facial expression.
— voice quality.
— general body tone.

**B.** My child's hobbies, outside interests include:
— reading, artwork, watching TV, movies.
— listening to music, playing instruments.
— sports, active games, handwork.

**C.** The part of school my child does best is:
— reading and writing.
— group discussion, music.
— gym, art, lab science.

**D.** When studying my child prefers:
— working alone; underlining, highlighting books and notes.
— working with someone else, asking and answering one another's questions.
— working alone for short periods of time interspersed with

_____ my child:

| | Visual | Auditory | Kinesthetic |
|---|---|---|---|
| (E.) my child: | either glares or looks away. | up volume of TV or stereo. | clenches fist, stamps out of room. |
| **F.** When explaining something, my child: | describes in detail; sees color, size, shape. | tells more than I ever knew before; repeats self. | gives minimum information, information has to be pried out. |
| **G.** When examining something new, my child: | moves closer to it, looks from every angle. | asks questions about it. | handles it, turns it over, wants to feel texture, weight. |
| **H.** In a social group, my child: | watches others, ceases talking when several others begin. | talks at the same time as others; talks louder as noise increases. | puts hands on others, moves frequently, suggests doing something. |
| **I.** When excited, my child: | demands my attention, some visible reaction; sentences get choppy. | talks rapidly, gives little or no time for response. | cannot stand or sit still, uses hand and arm movement. |
| **J.** When looking for encouragement or reward, my child: | looks for a smile, must have me see acomplishment. | needs verbal praise. | needs a hug, a pat on the back. |

**Total** _____ **Visual** _____ **Auditory** _____ **Kinesthetic**

## Interpreting the Results

Add the score in each of the three columns. Each of the three scores (which should total 100) is a percentage that indicates the relative strength of each of the modalities. A difference of plus or minus 5 points between two or even among all three modalities is not significant.

The greater the degree of strength in one area, the stronger that specific modality actually is. For example, if a person is found to have 50 percent in one specific area, quite obviously the two remaining areas must be divided between the

**Each child in a family will have his or her own learning strength.**

remaining 50 percent and are therefore weaker modes. If the other two modes are close to one another (each is close to 25 percent), the difference is great enough to make the dominant mode very apparent. If the other two modes are not evenly divided, the secondary mode will be closer to the dominant mode and thus more useful. The third mode will be weakest.

The following examples will help explain the interpretation of checklist scores. Table 2 presents the percentages of three children, Carrie, Justin, and Brook. Using the five-percentage-point criterion we recommend, Carrie would be termed primarily auditory with a secondary kinesthetic modality, Justin would have a dominant visual modality, and Brook would have mixed modality strengths.

Carrie's strongest modality is auditory. The difference between the kinesthetic and the visual is more than five points and, therefore, her secondary modality is kinesthetic. In working with Carrie, it would be logical for her parents to rely first on auditory input and then on kinesthetic input.

For Justin, the visual modality is obviously his strongest. The difference between the auditory and kinesthetic scores is not significant enough to determine a secondary modality. Justin will do well with visual examples, reminders, and rewards. If a parent or teacher gives him simply a verbal direction, he may forget or confuse what he was told.

Brook's scores were all within five points of each other, so he can be said to have mixed modality strengths. He is likely to benefit from material presented in any modality and to work with others regardless of their dominant modality.

| Table 2 | Visual | Auditory | Kinesthetic |
|---------|--------|----------|-------------|
| Carrie  | 25     | 42       | 33          |
| Justin  | 51     | 23       | 26          |
| Brook   | 33     | 31       | 36          |

Whatever your child's scores are, it is important to keep in mind that this checklist provides only an indication of what his or her strengths might be. The most reliable observations are those that have been made over an extensive period of time and in a variety of situations. Also, look beyond some of your initial observations of your child and see what might be reasons for his or her behavior. For instance, in elementary school almost every child's favorite time is recess. But is it actually because she is active and this is her time to run? Or does she talk to her friends, sing songs, repeat rhymes for jumping rope? Maybe she prefers to draw or set up a detailed scene for a game of pretending. At home almost all children watch some television. What do they pick up from it? Does your child hum a song he heard or repeat commercial phrases? Does he watch, always with something to hold onto or handle, possibly getting up frequently for a snack, to change position, to get a toy, or for no apparent reason at all? Does he notice detail? For example, does he notice an actor in one show who reappears as a different character in another show? There are many activities and behaviors common to all children, but the variations between children can tell a lot about particular learning styles.

Review your child's checklist and your own checklist with your spouse, another relative, or close friend. Our own observations of ourselves and our children may not be as objective as someone else's. The checklist also gives a clue to what to be sensitive for in the future. Now that you are more aware of what to watch for, you may find yourself noticing things you had overlooked.

Comparison of children's scores on the Swassing-Barbe Modality Index (a more formal modality assessment tool) also indicates that modality strengths may change. The relative strength of the visual and kinesthetic modalities increases between kindergarten and sixth grade, while the relative strength of audition is decreasing. Another shift may occur between the late elementary grades and adulthood. Thirty percent of the population remains visually dominant, but auditory skills are demanded more than kinesthetic ones.

Studies done on various groups with the Swassing-Barbe Modality Index show no significant differences between boys and girls, right- and left- handed people, or people of different races or ethnic backgrounds. Each child has his own learning strength, and it is not influenced by these variables.

## The Differences among Visual, Auditory, and Kinesthetic Children

The chapters that follow deal with the learning differences and teaching activities for each of the three types of learners. To help you get started on providing the right learning environment and experiences to match your child's learning strength, use the following chart. It will suggest to you the kinds of toys and activities each type of learner most enjoys.

If your modality is different from your child's, remember you are providing an environment for his or her learning strength, not yours. If you are a visual learner you may remember quiet, contented hours with crayons and paper as a child. Do not expect the same from your auditory or kinesthetic child who will either talk throughout or color several pages with abandon and be off on a new pursuit.

A colleague of mine was telling about one of her speaking engagements during which she noticed various members of the audience and how they exhibited certain modality behaviors—squirming in their seats, talking to themselves. One woman in particular who seemed to be especially visual caught her attention. This woman was very neat, sat perfectly still, and kept her eyes on the speaker the whole time. After the meeting the woman came up, absolutely furious. She was angry, not with the talk about modality strengths, but with her mother, who had ingrained in her the belief that ladies did not move in public. After hearing about modality, she now understood that she was kinesthetic, not visual. She had spent her energy controlling her need for physical movement. She had barely made it through school; she had not, and still did not, enjoy learning. The effort it took her to sit still did not allow her to learn as well as she could have.

# Toys and Activities for Each Learner

| | Visual | Auditory | Kinesthetic |
|---|---|---|---|
| Favorite Toys | Books, crayons, paints, puzzles; dolls to dress, dollhouse, figures to use for setting up scenes. | Records, cassettes, music boxes, instruments, dolls to talk to and talk for. | Manipulatives (nesting toys, rings, blocks), bikes, vehicles; dolls, figures to move to act out scenes. |
| Arts and Crafts Materials | Crayons, paints, chalk, etc. Enjoys scribbling from early age, staying in lines important as gets older. | Crayons, paints, chalk, etc. Will talk to self while drawing and be easily distracted by noises. | Durable crayons, paintbrushes; paper, paste, and scissors for cutting and pasting; large paper surfaces. |
| Pretend Play, Imagination | Visualizes in detail, likes to dress up. | Makes up conversations with self and others, announces roles and actions, makes vivid sound effects. | Very active, loves setting scenes and acting out in physical terms, dancing. |
| Water Play | Watches water while pouring and playing, enjoys sparkle on water and ripples. | Listens to different sounds of pouring from different containers and heights. | Splashes, kicks, washes, will jump in if possible. |
| Being Read to and Reading | Enjoys vivid description, beautiful and detailed illustrations. | Enjoys sounds of words, things with rhymes, alliteration, onomatopoeia. | Enjoys stories with action and adventure. |

*Chapter 4*

# Your Kinesthetic Child

"Erin is beginning to develop language ability, but she feels no need to use it. She has words for juice, cereal, and other things; but when she really wants something she will grab me and just point to whatever she wants. Sometimes she makes a game out of it, pointing to everything randomly, until I figure out the right one."               —Parent of a fifteen-month-old

"Patrick's goal in the tub has little to do with getting clean. When I give him a sponge or cloth, he washes down the walls, the tub *and* me. He loves to splash and kick! When we go swimming, Patrick spends as much time jumping in and out of the water as he does playing in it." —Parent of a three-year-old

"Jeff has developed a real dislike for school. He wakes up eagerly enough, but does everything he can to avoid getting dressed and out the door. His teacher complains that he never pays attention and is becoming a real troublemaker. She sends him to the principal, but when he gets there, he can't remember why he was sent. He's having a terrible time with every subject except art and physical education. But he can't tell me why. I'm afraid he will never do well in school."               —Parent of an eight-year-old

These children are demonstrating that they are kinesthetic learners. They are all physically active children, who literally throw themselves into things—even misbehaving. They don't waste time talking; they would rather be "doing." In fact, they would really like to "attack" problems, or "jump right in" and get started. We mean mentally, of course, but their first reaction is physical. They tend throughout life to act and then think.

If your child exhibits these tendencies and if the results of his checklist show him to be a kinesthetic learner, then your job as a parent and teacher should be physically active, too. You are going to have to participate in what your child is learning.

## Learning by Doing

You'll know your child is kinesthetic every time you try to put him in a snowsuit. He'll kick and squirm and wiggle, he's so ready to get going. He's the child who grows up with his shoes

**Always on the go, your kinesthetic child rarely notices her untied shoes.**

*Growing Up Learning*

untied. If the kinesthetic child can survive school, he can do very well in life. This is the child who learns by doing. He is full of energy and loves to take things apart to find out how they work. He wants to touch each part and manipulate it, so he can understand how it relates to the other parts.

Your kinesthetic child jumps for joy and hugs and kisses you lavishly when he is happy. On the other hand, he reacts physically when he is angry, too, punching and hitting, or at the very least, stomping off, rather than talking out his problem.

When he does talk, he uses his entire body to speak, gesturing, acting out, moving about. He has a hard time listening and quickly loses interest in details. He is eager to move on to something else.

If you put on some music he'll dance in response to the tune. If you take him to a museum, he tries to touch everything, much to your and the guards' dismay.

Your kinesthetic child is the most forgiving of all children. He will want any punishment to be over and done with, so he can put the misbehavior behind him and get on with life. He rarely worries about yesterday or tomorrow. Today is his adventure, and he is determined to make it so.

Energy *is* your kinesthetic child. It is what makes life with him exciting, but it is also what makes school difficult. Very few teachers know how to deal with so much energy in a room full of other children making demands on their time. When the teacher says, "Line up for lunch," the kinesthetic child is the first in line, or pushing everyone from the rear. If he can't lead, he'll push. How do you channel that energy into learning experiences when so many of the materials for teaching involve quiet listening and watching and memorizing?

Many parents, unfortunately, have the same problem. They have a difficult time keeping up with the kinesthetic child's high level of energy and activity. Problems may arise when the child uses physical outlets as attention-getting devices for a parent who is not as involved as the child would like. She may hit, grab, or get herself into danger just to "catch" her parent. Most of the time punishing or putting off such a child will only aggravate the problem. Make an effort to get involved for at least a short period of time each day. You can set a time limit;

your child can select the activity. Many times what you initiate the child can continue independently. Put on the radio and dance for five minutes. Dig tunnels and pile mountains in dirt or sand. Wrestle and pillow fight for a while. Help start constructing a wood project or model. Your child will love the time you spend playing together and, when you are finished, she can take off on her own.

Many a kinesthetic child is labeled "hyperactive" and put on medications that "quiet" her down. There is a great danger here, because if you deprive her of her energy, you are depriving her of her best opportunity to learn. If she can't learn by doing, she may very well stop caring about school at all. While there is such a thing as true hyperactivity, caution must be exercised whenever there is a question of putting children on medication.

## What You Can Do to Help at Home

Large muscles develop before small ones. Luckily, your child likes to use her large muscles, so provide her with as many opportunities as you can for developing them. Give her things to climb on, run around, and take apart. A climbing dome is a relatively inexpensive, safe, yard toy that very young children can quite easily master, without the danger of long falls. Bicycles, jump ropes, roller skates, balls, and whatever your local park or your own outside play area can offer will give her happy hours of learning the way she does best.

Inside, be sure that you have a big blackboard and lots of colored chalk for scribbling, writing, and drawing. Give her large spaces on which to create. Finger paints and long sheets of shelf paper, mounds of clay or play dough—these are materials she will delight in.

She will also enjoy acting out plays, so a large box or basket of "dress up" articles is a must, along with dolls, trucks, action figures, big wooden blocks, and puppets. Supply large containers to keep her toys in, and she will be just as happy to put them away as to take them out. When you are showing her how to put things away, let her be in charge of the big toys. You put away the tiny ones.

In her own room, keep things simple. If you can, provide hooks for her clothes at a level she can reach, rather than

**Shared physical activities—no matter where or when—are especially important for kinesthetic children.**

hangers high in a closet. She will hang her clothes up quite contentedly on hooks.

What happens on rainy days when your active child can't get outside to run off that energy? Here is what one clever mother did:

"One rainy, inside day, Stephen was itching for something to do since he couldn't go outside and run around. We ended up cleaning the entire kitchen together. I got out a pan of water and a sponge for him. Stephen would stand on a chair, clean one portion of the counter, climb down, move the chair, climb up and clean another portion of the counter, and so on until he'd reached everything. There was water all over, but Stephen had a real sense of accomplishment. He had used some energy, and the only mess was water which would dry in time. Stephen actually enjoys dusting, washing windows, vacuuming, and sweeping."

It is important for you to remember, as this mother did,

that the goal is not cleaning. Don't be critical of your child and his degree of success. Congratulate him for really making a great effort! You'll be channeling his need to "do" into learning to keep the house clean.

## Discipline

Your kinesthetic child will not respond well to verbal discussions or admonitions when he has done something wrong. Teachers have discovered this when they send a kinesthetic child to the principal. By the time he gets there, he often has forgotten the reason for which he was sent. Moreover, simply getting sent out of the classroom means an opportunity to be out of his chair and walking—or running—down the hall! In fact, any punishment quickly wears off. It is much better to divert the child from what he is doing wrong to what he does right.

If, however, a kinesthetic child does something dangerous, like running out into the street, don't shout at him. Pick him up forcibly, if he is small, and carry him away from the scene of his crime. Your angry physical presence will be enough to emphasize that what he has done is wrong.

In other situations needing discipline—a child hitting, grabbing, misbehaving—the clearest message for the kinesthetic child is to be removed from what he is doing. Set aside a "time out" spot where the child is to sit quietly until he is told he can get up. Interrupting his activity will frequently get the message across. Do not make the "time out" excessively long, and make sure the child knows the reason for the discipline in the first place; then allow him to return to what he was doing before.

## Rewards

The best way to reward a kinesthetic learner is to hug or pat him while telling him what a great job he has done. He will respond best to your physical show of happiness and satisfaction. Another strategy is to reward a job completed or an assignment done well with some sort of physical activitity to be shared by you both. For example, if he gets his homework done you can play ball together. He not only gets the activity he loves, he gets you in the deal as well!

**"Great job!" and a pat on the back are the kinesthetic learner's rewards.**

To structure tasks for success, it is helpful for you to demonstrate to your kinesthetic learner what you want done. Verbal requests or directions alone may not get the results you want.

In thinking about how well you and your child do together, it might be helpful for you to compare the responses on your parent checklist with the responses on your child's checklist. Are you perhaps giving him verbal praise when he needs a reassuring touch? When you have some free time with your child, do you share an active game or a hands-on project that he might want, or do you suggest something to your liking?

Of course, there will be times when the last thing you have to share is energy. You wouldn't mind giving your child some time if only it could be quiet time. Try to think of ways you can meet his needs without making excessive demands on yourself. If you read a book with him, make it a story that is filled with action. Ask him questions about the story that let him feel he is

**Pow! You wouldn't want to deprive him of his zest for doing and learning!**

part of the action. If possible, you might even ask him to act out parts of the story as you read along. If he wants to run outside, you can pretend to be the timekeeper at the Olympic trials and make up different races for him to try—running, hopping, skipping, going forward, going backward, the possibilities are endless. He enjoys the activity and you get to sit still with a stopwatch!

Whatever strategies you find, remember to reward him for his energy, not punish him or confine him in an effort to control it. That would only go against his natural abilities and undermine his zest for doing and learning.

## At School

If your child is already in school, you can help right now. Talk to his teacher. Tell him or her of your observations about how your child learns and discuss what the teacher has observed. Teachers will recognize kinesthetic learners as the ones who are always asking to go to the bathroom and to sharpen their pencils, two of the only acceptable reasons for moving around during classtime. A kinesthetic learner's pencil is only two inches long by nine o'clock in the morning! Not only that, he also presses harder on the pencil when writing, wearing it down faster or breaking the point more frequently.

If your child has been having trouble learning in school, ask the teacher how you can reinforce his subjects at home. Remember, our goal here is to fortify your child's learning strength, not practice his weaknesses while hoping to change them through repetition. As a parent, you can help "translate" the subjects he is having trouble with into the "doing" kind of language he understands. Continue watching your child and keep his teacher informed about any potential problem areas you may observe. If his teacher and you both understand kinesthetic teaching strategies you can head off problems before they start.

## The Point of Intervention

"If at first you don't succeed, try, try again, *but in a different way*" could well be the motto of modality-based instruction.

If your child doesn't understand easily the way you first present a new concept, alter your teaching strategy. We call this the "point of intervention." This is the time when your child is really saying, "I don't understand the way you have just taught the lesson. Teach it in a way that I can understand."

It is natural that we repeat what we have just said, only louder or more slowly. But this won't work so a new strategy is needed. At school the teacher will probably group your child with others with the same modality strength who have not grasped that particular lesson. At home you will have to give him another way to learn.

## Reading

Reading is primarily a visual skill, involving the ability to look at a word and understand it. Your kinesthetic child may, therefore, have a difficult time learning to read.

The earlier you share time reading, the better off your kinesthetic child will be. She may not want to sit for long, but even when she is one, two, and three, you can offer very short books with thick pages just right for her short attention span. In the beginning, don't even worry about the story the book tells. The kinesthetic child will go through a book just to turn the pages, which is fine. Many publishers now have books that "pop up" when you open a page, or that have push-pull tabs to make the pictures move, and windows to open to reveal hidden things. Be careful with these books around very young children, though. They may try to take the book apart! When your child is sitting with you long enough to get the idea of a story, make sure you select books that have lots of action, preferably right in the very beginning.

**At any age, the kinesthetic learner may prefer just to turn pages —and that's fine.**

You can help her at home by emphasizing the left-to-right and top-to-bottom progressions so important in reading. These can be taught through large and small muscle activities. For example, put several objects on her left. Ask her to pick up one item on her left and move it to the right. Repeat the direction until all the objects are on her right. As she moves an item you might repeat "left to right" if the added auditory input will support the movement. The objects can be large, like a wastebasket, a cardboard box, or a big ball, so your child has to stand to move them from one side to another. Or the objects can be smaller and she can move them along the top of a table or desk. If she has an easel or chalkboard you can put a strip of sandpaper along the left side of it for her to use as a starting point when drawing lines. The same procedure can be used for top-to-bottom progression by putting the sandpaper along the top.

Finger pointing is a strategy which helps the kinesthetic child focus on the appropriate word. This has often been discouraged but our research shows that pointing, preferably with the index and middle finger, really helps. The width of two fingers "underlines" whole words, rather than single letters, and involves the child physically in the act of reading. Writing letters on her big blackboard and drawing imaginary letters in the air will also help.

There are a number of reading games you can make with or for your kinesthetic child to encourage indirect physical involvement in reading. In these games the child imagines she is participating in an event, such as holding a baseball while reading a baseball story.

"Surfboard" is a game that can be played with words. On a large piece of paper draw a series of waves. Above each wave

**Finger pointing helps the reader focus on whole words and physically involves him in reading.**

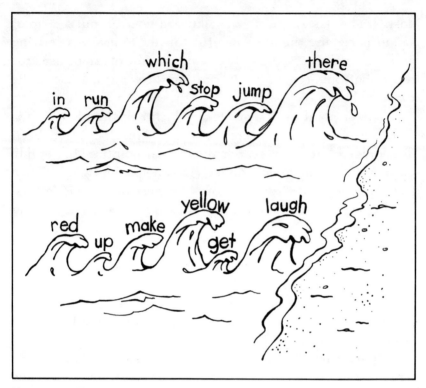

**You can make a number of reading games to match your child's interests.**

write a word, hard words on big waves and easier ones on small waves. The child's task is to "ride" the waves to the beach. If the child misses a word, she has "fallen off the surfboard" and must find a new wave to ride, until she can reach the beach. This game can be varied in any number of ways to match the area in which you live or any interest your child has. Your child can "Climb the Mountain," "Cross the Desert," even "Conquer Outer Space" by going from planet to planet or star to star, until a destination is reached.

For many children, the trick to reading is motivation. When your child is older, she may know how to read, but not do it much at all. To help in this respect, you can actually make it a trick! A number of "magic" tricks, optical illusions, and other games are included on pp. 157-158. You can write the directions to one trick on a card, or have your child read it in the book. If she can read the trick, then she can perform it. If sleight of hand is not the motivation that catches your child, see what will work.

A new recipe for cookies that you might help her bake (as *she* reads the directions), an article in a magazine about a topic or person she likes, newspaper reviews of upcoming movies she might like to see—there are many ways to bring reading into her world.

## Handwriting

Your kinesthetic child can excel at handwriting, since it is essentially a kinesthetic task. Your child will enjoy tracing, motioning, and writing on her blackboard. You write or make the motions of the letters and have your child copy them. Do the

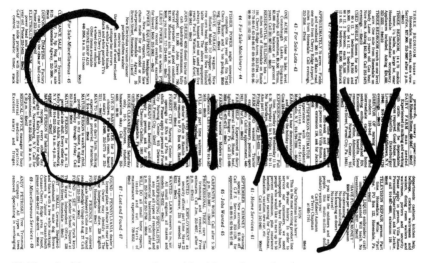

**Writing in big spaces such as blackboards and newspapers encourages large muscle development.**

same with numbers. If you don't have a blackboard, use the classified section of your newspaper. Turn it sideways and have your child write letters and numerals on the big columns which are separated by the spaces.

Kinesthetic children love things with texture, and this is another tool you can use to help them learn. Sandpaper letters or cards with letters in relief will give kinesthetic children a "feel" for the letters and their shapes.

Your child will have more difficulty writing in small spaces, so encourage her to practice in large spaces. She may also push

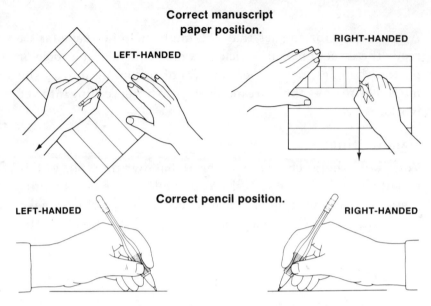

**Correct manuscript paper position.**

LEFT-HANDED  RIGHT-HANDED

**Correct pencil position.**

LEFT-HANDED  RIGHT-HANDED

too hard on her pencil or pen when concentrating. Help her to relax by providing big places to write, and show her how to use correct pencil and paper position.

## Arithmetic

Much arithmetic depends upon memorization. Once the child has mastered the basic rules, he can readily adapt them to more advanced mathematics. So your role at home will be to provide manipulative or "hands-on" materials to help him be physically involved in the processes of arithmetic. There are quite a number of commercial products available, like an abacus or Cuisenaire rods. But even simple old-fashioned flash cards are helpful. You can make these, or let your child make them, by cutting out pieces of paper or using 3 x 5 cards and writing addition, subtraction, multiplication, and division facts upon them. Have your child start with one pile. As he learns a particular fact, have him put that card into another pile. He can even carry those he knows in his left pocket and those he does not in his right. Or you can put the pile of those he knows on one side of the room, and the ones he does not on the other. As he learns the fact, let him get up and take the card to the pile he knows. This motion will help involve him and reinforce his memory.

For learning many different arithmetic facts a system

called Chisanbop may help kinesthetic children through finger manipulations. For a complete explanaton and description of Chisanbop you might read the *Complete Book of Chisanbop: Original Finger Calculation Method* (Van Nostrand Reinhold, 1981).

Always remember, the kinesthetic learner understands initial arithmetic skills best when numbers are presented as concrete objects that he can handle and manipulate. With practice and the normal development of his learning skills, your kinesthetic child should be able to deal with abstract numbers just as well as visual and auditory learners.

## Spelling

The easiest and best way for your kinesthetic child to learn his spelling words is to write them. His blackboard and unlined paper are the best surfaces upon which to practice. Writing the words large, using large muscles, is more effective than writing them small. Sometimes writing with different instruments—pencils, pens, crayons—helps to reinforce his learning because he can *feel* the word.

**Every opportunity to touch, feel, and manipulate, is a learning opportunity.**

Plastic, magnetized letters of the alphabet are also a good source for learning spelling. Your child can feel each letter and the entire word as he arranges it on his board or on your refrigerator door.

There are several tricks that help kinesthetic learners distinguish left from right and between letters such as *b* and *d*, and *p* and *q*. Kinesthetic learners can form these letters physically to make it easier to visualize differences. For *b* and *d*, have them make a loose fist with both hands, putting their thumbs straight up and turning the fists so they can see their four fingernails. The left hand represents the *b*, and the right hand, the *d*. For *p* and *q*, they turn their fists down. (See illustration.)

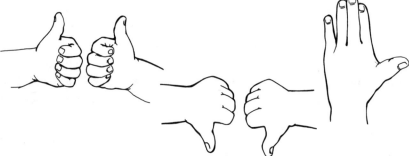

For a left-right reminder, have kinesthetic children put their fingers out straight and together, thumbs pointing to each other, and turn their wrists so they can see the backs of their hands. Their left hand forms the letter *L* for *Left*.

## Lifetime Study Habits

Parents can help teachers by helping their own children "learn to learn" or study subjects taught at school. As we have pointed out in each of the methods for learning basic skills, the kinesthetic child learns by doing. This will apply to more advanced subjects as she matures. You will find that she will do well in "lab" sciences because they involve doing. But social studies, literature, and everything else can also be mastered by your kinesthetic child if she learns how to use her learning strength to aid her in mastering skills usually learned through another sensory mode.

One of the most remarkable instances of matching

**With the help of parent and teacher, your kinesthetic child can use his learning strength successfully to master all his subjects.**

teaching strategies to learning strengths involved the son of an elementary school principal. The boy's father had made a great issue of behaving well in class, being quiet and still. The boy, Randy, was in second grade and had a severe reading dysfunction. He was tested for learning strengths and shown to be very strongly kinesthetic. He was not auditory or visual. He did not have any perceptual disabilities; he simply could not retain information presented in either form. His teacher called on every kinesthetic teaching strategy she knew. Randy began using finger movements; he manipulated word cards; he tracked his reading with his fingers. He was given time at the chalkboard and with paper and large markers to write and read what he had written. After a few weeks Randy was making fine progress and well on his way to realizing his potential as a very bright child.

Actually, as a toddler, Randy had provided clues to his modality strength and weaknesses, which his parents could have picked up on had they known what to look for. His father remembered that, at family gatherings when there were lots of people and noise, Randy would run around, put both hands on his ears, and say "No talk, no talk." With the modality testing scores and behavior observations, Randy's parents and teacher realized that too much auditory input was stressful to him. Given kinesthetic resources and an almost sterile auditory environment, Randy was not only capable of learning but enjoyed the progress he made. As he gains confidence in his ability and understanding of his learning style, his teacher and his parents can slowly work on developing his visual and auditory modalities to enable him to function in any situation. The key is to strengthen his weaker modalities through the use of his dominant modality. In this way he will acquire skills that he can use throughout his life.

Teach your kinesthetic learner to "take apart" her lessons and make study tools that she can actually hold. Flash cards, which can be transferred from a pile she does not know to one she does know, will continue to be good learning tools. And whenever you can, take her to a museum or a living history area, where she can "walk around" information and take it in from all sides. Encourage her to make a drama of history, a laboratory of science, a sport of literature. The strategies you use to help with early reading, writing, arithmetic, and spelling will help her learn all her life.

*Chapter 5*

# Your Auditory Child

"Matthew loves to play hide-and-seek. It is all right for me to know where he is hiding. He likes to listen as I describe each place I look. 'Is he under the sofa? No, he's not there. Could he be behind the chair? No, not there. I don't know where he could be. I've looked in the closet, in the oven, in the refrigerator, under the table. I've looked everywhere!' Then he pops out and surprises me with much noise and commotion."　　　　— Parent of a two-year-old

"Julie has started to imitate me spelling words aloud when I don't want her to know what I'm saying. She picks random letters and makes up spellings, but that is how she asks for things that are sometimes forbidden. For example, she may say, 'If I eat all my lunch, can I have some *a-s-t-s*?' That's her attempt at *s-o-d-a*."　　　　— Parent of a four-year-old

"Ellen loves her piano lessons. She sometimes plays the piano to release tension when she is angry or upset. She bangs out every emotion inside her, sometimes actually making up tunes to express herself. She has always loved music and frequently whistles as she strolls down the street. I can hear her coming."　　　　— Parent of a nine-year-old

These children are auditory learners. They talk and sing, whistle and hum, shout their joy or anger, listening to all that life has to offer them. They learn what they hear.

If your child exhibits these tendencies and if the results of his checklist show him to be an auditory learner, then your job as a parent and teacher will involve much listening and talking, too, even if you are not an auditory learner yourself.

**Your auditory child must hear what she reads to learn it. The quieter she can be, the less she will disrupt others.**

## Learning by Listening

Your auditory child is a talker. He is the one who might disturb other students in his class by reading his lesson out loud when he thinks he is reading to himself. He needs to hear what he is reading in order to learn it.

When your auditory child is learning new words you will frequently hear him repeat words and phrases to himself in order to store them away for future use. More than other children he will pick up the tone and pitch of a parent's angry or tired voice and use the same tone later in his own speech. He will often sound like a little echo!

He asks questions constantly and is not satisfied with "I don't know." He will keep asking until he gets an answer. He is also not happy if you tell him to "look it up" rather than talk the answer out with him. He explores things by talking about them.

Your auditory child gets louder when he is frustrated. If you don't listen to him or don't understand, he says it more loudly. He expresses his emotions verbally, just changing his tone or the pitch of his voice. He actually can work out his anger through loud words. But he soon calms down. He can talk out his problems, trying various solutions verbally. He will talk to anyone, and whether they listen or not makes little difference. If no one is around, he talks to himself.

You will often find your auditory child mumbling to himself when he is working on a puzzle or playing with a toy or trying to fix something. He will grumble his way to a solution.

Auditory learners enjoy listening, but they cannot wait to talk themselves, interrupting in their eagerness to be heard.

At the end of the day be prepared to hear a long, repetitive description of everything that happened to your child. She likes the sound of her voice, and she is putting the events of her day into perspective by telling you about them. She will also want to talk about what is going to happen tomorrow before she goes to bed. This is her way of getting ready for what she must face in the morning. She wants to think it out ahead of time.

When your child gets involved in new activities and sports she will talk about what to do, how to do it, why it's done that way. An associate of mine was relating stories about her three grandchildren, including her six-year-old grandson. He was learning to swim, and having more than the usual problems because he was trying to talk himself into learning the movements required. He was so auditory he could not master the rhythm of the strokes he was supposed to make without saying it aloud. You can imagine the predicament he found himself in!

Your auditory child loves music in all its forms, from banging on a can or pounding pot lids together to all the adult music you enjoy. She won't be as responsive to visual arts, but she will be happy to talk about what she sees, sometimes missing the details but understanding the picture as a whole.

**Even an impromptu kitchen serenade is music to his ears!**

She may miss nuances of color, but she will gladly try to tell you as much as she can.

You may receive a report card saying that your auditory child has been talking in class, disrupting classmates. But you and her teacher must be careful not to repress her talking too much, or you will be depriving her of her best opportunity to learn. If she cannot talk and listen to others talking, she may not learn as much as she is able.

At home, nonauditory parents may find a child who is very auditory to be disruptive, even frustrating. Parents may want a period of "peace and quiet" only to find themselves repeatedly harassed by questions, requests, stories, and announcements. Try giving your child your undivided listening attention for a set period of time. When you need your time for quiet, channel her audition by suggesting she make up stories with her animals and dolls. Or put on a record or tape for her to listen to (even providing her with headphones if you have them).

However, there will be many times when nothing will substitute for you when your child is working on something. One visual/kinesthetic mother felt she was going crazy with her son's constant talking. The mother's approach was to list things on paper to organize herself or simply to attack problems by doing whatever was close at hand. Her son was always asking, "What will happen if . . .? What if I do this . . . how about that . . .? Why will that happen?" Through all the questions it seemed to this mother that her child took forever to *do* anything. Once she realized he needed this kind of interaction, it made it a little easier for her to accept him and not try to change him. Instead of insisting he just *do* something and stop the talk, she made the effort to have more patience, to listen a little more, and then lead him into trying what he had been discussing. This mother was taking the first step in allowing her child to grow according to his own gifts.

## What You Can Do to Help At Home

Children learn to make loud noises before soft ones, so give your auditory child as many opportunities as you can to talk, sing, listen, and shout, in constructive settings. Records and tapes to listen to and sing with, inexpensive musical toys or ones you can make together out of cans and pans, combs and whistles—these are the best learning instruments you can give your child. There are many excellent educational records and tapes on the market. Edmunds Scientific , for instance, makes a series called "Little Thinker Tapes" for ages three to about eight, which cover all sorts of topics from poetry to dinosaurs and weather. Each tape comes with a blank book of paper that children can make drawings in, as the tape suggests. These tapes will provide your auditory child with hours of constructive play and knowledge. They may be available at your library and at good toy stores or you can send for them through the Edmunds Scientific Co., 101 East Glouster Pike, Barrington, NJ, 08007. With the advent of inexpensive tape decks there are hundreds of materials available for auditory children.

**Close "friends" may be included in play—if they are willing to listen and follow directions.**

Dolls and stuffed toys will make good "listeners" when your auditory child is playing alone. She will enjoy making up conversations among her playthings and friends, acting out long dialogues and plays.

While she paints and draws, she will talk to herself about what she is creating. Her drawings will be stories, and she will delight in telling you all about them, giving each character a different voice and making vivid sound effects. Listen to her stories and ask questions to help her develop her thoughts and imaginings.

Even while you are driving along in the car, your auditory child can learn. You and she can play "listening games" that will sharpen her auditory skills and keep the entire family occupied. *Listening Games for Elementary Grades* by Margaret John Maxwell (Acropolis Books, Washington, D.C.) contains fun games for ages three to twelve that can be played almost anywhere. Several of them are described on pages 141-142. Your auditory child is already "all ears"; these games will help your child focus her auditory skill.

Your local librarian and your child's teacher can give you suggestions for many other auditory materials to strengthen and reinforce the way your child learns best.

## Discipline

Your auditory child will respond to verbal discussions and admonitions. But take care to keep verbal discipline and lectures as brief as necessary to make your point. If you continue on for too long the auditory child may stop listening altogether and your point will be lost. On the other hand, you may find yourself

Caught in the act! But you can be sure your auditory child will have a "good" explanation.

"caught" by him at times in long debates going around and around the point in question. A man I know was airing some of his frustrations about rearing his two children. He felt he was primarily auditory, and when he gave his kinesthetic daughter a reprimand or request, she followed through almost immediately, and went on about her business. His frustration came in dealing with his son, who was also auditory. The two of them would hook each other in verbal combat. He described his son as always "talking him under the table" about why he will or will not do something, never afraid to say what he thinks.

If you find yourself in a similar predicament, keep two thoughts in mind. First, make sure you and your child define the problem so that both of you understand and agree on what is being discussed, keeping it to one issue at a time. Second, let your child be part of the problem-solving process. Ask him for ideas on appropriate actions or reasonable solutions. It may require some give-and-take between you to find an answer that is acceptable to both (and at times, there is no answer acceptable to him); but being a part of the process makes the final decision less dogmatic and teaches him responsibility for his actions.

When the auditory child is angry, you may find he gets louder and louder. Help him to tell you why he is angry, "only more softly this time." His anger is quickly spent in loud words, and then you can verbally reason together in softer tones. Through conversation you can let him describe the problem from his point of view and possibly come up with his own solution.

One mother recently complained to me that she was always scolding her son for interrupting her conversations with friends when they came to visit. I suggested she have the child tell her friend, right at the beginning, about something he has recently done. This would give him the verbal attention he craves, and his mother could then direct him on to another activity. An auditory child likes to be heard from. If you don't let him talk in the beginning, he is going to interrupt you until he has a chance to talk.

## Rewards

The best way to reward your auditory child is to tell her what she did right and explain why. She needs verbal praise and reinforcement. Be aware that your auditory child will also pick up on your tone of voice. Praise that *sounds* honest, not just muttered distractedly, will mean the most. When she is really looking for encouragement, it is important that you push back the problems, chores, and other concerns you have and praise her in words *and* expression.

Another reward for positive behavior is to share an activity that your child enjoys. Do not let anything interrupt or postpone that time. Let your child plan it, and make sure she understands that this in particular is in response to an achievement or behavior that you are proud of.

Give some thought to how well you and your spouse interact with your auditory child. Compare your answers on the modality checklist with those of your child's. The behaviors of an auditory child can frequently be misread by someone nonauditory and may result in discipline instead of reward from a person who does not understand this child's learning style.

Kyle is a boy who takes in absolutely everything he hears, whether it appears he is paying attention or not. His neighbor asked him to care for her kitten while she was away. She gave very detailed instructions, but became angry when she felt Kyle had not been listening. She demanded he repeat her directions, and she was astonished when he did—almost word for word. The problem had arisen because Kyle does not give much eye contact to a person who is talking. Many people misinterpret his behavior and scold him when actually he has done an excellent job of listening.

The same problem arose in school one year when Kyle's teacher notified his parents that he appeared to have a learning problem. The problem was not reflected in his grades, but his teacher was concerned. Again, the teacher's style demanded eye contact and, when Kyle did not attend visually, the teacher didn't understand that Kyle could learn without it.

A related situation occurred with the son of a co-worker. Chris was an auditory learner who had been diagnosed as learning disabled. He told one high school teacher that the teacher had a very interesting voice, and he liked to listen to it. He could listen even better, in fact, with his head down. The teacher was skeptical, but having been so complimented, decided to let Chris try listening that way. Chris learned the oral material much better than usual, and the teacher let him continue listening with his head down. Without realizing quite what they had done, the teacher and student had accepted a strategy that allowed Chris to focus his auditory strength while screening out visual distractions.

To some students, input in a weak modality can act as a stress or interference, actually inhibiting learning. This is an area of modality education we have only begun to look at and something that needs more research before we fully understand how modality interference works and what children it affects.

## At School

Talk to your child's teacher about what you have observed. Find out what his teacher has discovered, and ask how you can reinforce teaching at home. If his only problem is talking too much, he can learn to subvocalize more. Since much current teaching material is geared to auditory and visual learners, he may have no other problems with school. But if he is having trouble with any one of his subjects, try to find out how it is being taught. Perhaps it is not being presented to him in the way he learns best—orally.

## The Point of Intervention

"The point of intervention" is that time when a child does not understand a concept or lesson the way it is first presented. For an auditory child, this means visual or kinesthetic material may have been presented without sufficient verbal directions. At this point the teaching strategy needs to be changed to include auditory material that will appeal to the child's modality strength. Verbal repetition will be helpful, and in some cases may be all that is necessary to make the lesson easier to understand. For younger children, putting words, phrases, and numbers into songs or chants adds an aspect that is helpful and fun, too. For older children, a discussion may be needed to define concepts, arrange steps in a process, clarify the unknown. Your insight into your own child and how he learns will help dictate how the material should be presented to be most effective.

## Reading

You should have no trouble getting your preschool child interested in books. Auditory children love language and all its possibilities. From the time they are babies, they delight in nursery rhymes, songs, tongue twisters, almost anything you read aloud. When you read to your auditory child, she may like to close her eyes if it helps her concentrate. You'll find she enjoys the sounds of words, and will delight in hearing stories like Dr. Seuss books, which are filled with imaginative words. Poetry with its rhymes, alliteration, and onomatopoeia will also be good reading material for the two of you.

When your child is a little older, encourage her to develop

comprehension skills by asking her to tell you about a story she has just heard. To draw the connection between the spoken word and the written word, ask your child to dictate a sentence or a whole story for you to write in big letters. Then the two of you can reread what she has dictated. This is a nice idea to use for a parent who must come home after the child has gone to bed or who must be away for a period of time. Have her dictate sentences about what she does each day to save and share when the family is back together. If you also have a child who is visual or kinesthetic, ask him or her to illustrate what the auditory child dictates!

**Dictating sentences can help your child understand the connection between the spoken and written words.**

You can develop the association between letters and sounds by playing rhyming games or alliteration games in the course of the day. Take turns saying a word, then providing a word that rhymes with it. Or pick a letter of the alphabet and work together to build a nonsense sentence using words that start with that letter.

When your child reaches school, or if she is in school already, ask her teacher about the reading program being used. Many schools teach reading through phonics. If your child's school follows this practice, she is probably having little trouble learning to read. She may have difficulty, however, reading to herself. She'll be saying the words out loud, so she can "hear" them better. You can help her sound out words at home, and learn to "say" them to herself. Auditory readers also tend to simply skip words they don't know and descriptive passages that don't interest them. They can often be slow readers, even though good ones, because they subvocalize every word. But don't discourage your child from either subvocalizing or moving her lips when reading. These things reinforce her reading and are important to her understanding of what she is learning. Just be certain the vocalizing is not so loud that it disturbs others.

## Handwriting

Handwriting, because it is primarily a kinesthetic activity, may be difficult for your child in the beginning. He will tend to write lightly and to say the strokes as he makes them.

You can help him at home by giving oral directions on how to make the letters he is practicing. Say the sound of the letter and have him write it, tell him the letter name and have him explain to you how he is going to write it. Let him say these instructions out loud as he constructs each letter. For example, lower-case letter t would be *pull down straight; lift; slide right.* All manuscript letters are made up of six basic strokes: pull down straight, slide right, circle back, circle forward, slant right, and slant left. In working with an auditory child on handwriting, it is important that you be consistent in the language you use to describe letters, strokes, line quality, and so on. Nothing is more frustrating to the person who depends upon auditory cues than having these cues change whimsically.

## Arithmetic

Arithmetic is another skill area that is well adapted to modality-based teaching; but there are more materials available for kinesthetic learners than for any other group. Repetition of tables and rules, however, is the auditory learner's most effective way to learn fundamental mathematics operations. After they have said the rules repeatedly and learned them, auditory learners begin to understand what they mean and can apply them.

Verbal practice of addition, subtraction, multiplication, and division facts at home with your child will be your most valuable contribution to her understanding of arithmetic. And talking through an arithmetic problem from beginning to end will help her understand and remember the process better than anything else you can do.

## Spelling

Auditory learners often do much better in spelling bees than they do on written spelling tests. They like spelling bees and learn from saying the words aloud and hearing others spell the words. They learn by how a word sounds, not what it looks like. The same phonics skills that help them in reading can be adapted to spelling. Your best approach at home will be saying the correct pronunciation of a word as your child listens, helping her count the syllables and listen for the sounds of vowels and diphthongs. You'll find your auditory child saying the sounds of a word as she writes it. Let her say the sounds, but make sure that she knows how to write those sounds. Auditory learners sometimes spell a word with the correct number of syllables, but they may leave out a silent letter.

> Most salmon, that are heading for
> for the ocean die when they try to get throo
> man-made, resirvwar, or else they get
> eaten by birds and other fish. The saman
> that get to the sea stay for six months,
> to five years. They feed on shrimp, squid,
> and small fish. Salmon spawn during
> summer and autum after swimming
> upstream as far as 2,000 miles from
> the ocean. This jurnee may take several
> months.

**Auditory learners will rely on sound when spelling words. Notice the phonetic approach to "throo," "autum," and "jurnee."**

## Lifetime Study Habits

All of the activities we have been discussing will help your child learn to learn his best way—auditorily. If he can learn to apply his auditory strengths to each new concept he has to master, you will have helped him immeasurably.

By the time he reaches secondary school with its dependence on lectures, he should have no trouble. You can help him reinforce lecture learning by taking notes *after* he has listened, not trying to take down every word. Some teachers will permit students to tape their lectures. For your auditory child, listening to a tape of the lecture, rather than reading through copious notes, is going to be a much better way for him to study. Encourage him to ask his teachers if he can tape their lessons. Foreign languages that are taught conversationally and through repetition of tapes will be much easier for him than those taught through reading and writing first.

One very bright auditory child has devised a method of studying for tests that suits her strengths perfectly. Amy assembles questions about the material and gives them to her mother to read aloud. Amy then answers the questions aloud. If she does not know the answer, her mother tells it to her and they go on. At the end of the set of questions Amy always says, "Ask me again. I want to make sure I know." Even when she gets all the answers right, the two of them may go through this process three or four times until Amy is confident about all the material. While this method of studying may seem worthless to someone visual or kinesthetic, it works for Amy who is one of the top students in her class.

Amy knows herself well enough to understand what works for her. By talking and listening, Amy learns a subject thoroughly and can then write the material for a test. With your help and that of the teacher, your auditory child will find the particular strategies that work for her. Support her in this effort, and she will be rewarded with a sense of confidence and achievement all her life.

*Chapter 6*

# Your Visual Child

"Maria starts to cry when I discipline her. Then she stops and looks at me, studying my facial expression hard and long to see if I still look stern and angry or if I have relaxed and am smiling again. If I am still angry, she may start crying again, intermittently checking my expression until she feels it's okay."

— Parent of an eighteen-month-old

"When Josh wants my attention, I can't just listen and go on with what I am doing. He comes right up to me and takes my face in his hands, putting himself practically nose to nose with me and then he will tell me what is on his mind. Eye contact seems to be critical to his communicating with me."

— Parent of a four-year-old

"Kathy is a very quiet, obedient child. Her teacher tells me that she knows the answers to questions, but never blurts them out. Her teacher has to call on her. She loves to draw and read, and seldom gets involved in the noisy games other children seem to prefer. She is a dreamer."

— Parent of a seven-year-old

These children are visual learners. To them the world is a series of pictures which they must see to understand. They are often quiet, careful people, who watch what is going on around them before they participate. Their faces are full of life, crying easily or bright with smiles. You can tell what they are thinking or feeling just by looking at them.

If your child is like this and if the responses on her checklist showed her to be a visual learner, then your job as a parent and teacher is going to involve helping her "see" the world around her.

## Learning by Seeing

Your visual child is a watcher. She learns best by watching demonstrations or by focusing on the details and components of a new concept. She won't always be able to remember the name of a new friend; but she'll be able to describe that friend's appearance with accuracy and insight, often identifying one physical characteristic that sets that child apart.

If you take your visual child into a new place, she will immediately look at and study everything in the room. She is

**For your visual child, daydreaming is thoughtful activity full of images.**

quick to notice similarities and differences and to draw comparisons to familiar objects. A chair might be just like one in her house, a room might be the same color as hers. When she goes to play at a friend's house she will immediately see which toys are like hers and which are different.

Visual learners tend to be neat; they appreciate tidiness and order because they are easily distracted by visual disorder or movement. They actually concentrate better when the space around them is visually "tidy." Yet they have vivid imaginations, full of pictures and colorful details.

You'll have to "draw" out your visual learner. She isn't a great talker, and she may stare off into space, daydreaming, when asked to sit and listen for a long time. She may use words clumsily when describing something new, but that doesn't mean she doesn't understand it. She is "seeing" it quite clearly in her mind's eye.

She tends to be a deliberating thinker, who likes to plan things out in advance. When she knows how to write, she will spend a great deal of time organizing thoughts on paper, listing problems and things she has to do, so she won't forget anything.

Visual learners enjoy artwork of all kinds. They draw pictures to show what they mean. They create detailed picture stories, with each leaf drawn meticulously on every tree and

**Eyelashes, jacket and boot detail, apples in the tree, and butterfly antennae are indications of visual artists at work!**

every eyelash noted on characters. They often insist that people look at something they are talking about, or they ask "Do you see?" meaning "Do you understand?"

If neither you nor your child's teacher is a visual learner, you may have trouble communicating with your child. You won't understand why he can't tell you what is wrong or why he doesn't always speak up in class when he knows the answer. Let him write it all down for you or draw you a picture. He will communicate his thoughts and feelings better with words you (and he) can see on paper.

Visual children are usually slower than others to begin talking when they are young. One grandfather I know wondered whether his grandson was retarded because the boy had not started speaking as early as the other grandchildren had. This notion may be common among auditory learners but it is a complete fallacy. What visual children are taking in is simply less measurable than the language exhibited by auditory children or the actions of kinesthetic children. They are receiving information and storing it away in their mind's eye, and when they are ready they will begin to use words to describe what they have learned. But for them, talking is simply not so important as observing.

**"Let me see!" Catching a bug presents a wonderful opportunity for detailed study. A book on insects can expand this new interest.**

Those who do not share this child's visual strength may become impatient at his insistence to "Show Me!" and "Look at this!" It may be that he has found something he has never seen before—he wants to see it up close, and he wants you to study it with him. He may have painted a new picture, written his name, or created a story, and he must have you look at his achievement. Or it may even be something you are doing, whether new or quite ordinary, that he needs to see, too, in order to know. Take the time to show him, as long as you are able. Sometimes he will need only a short time to see as much he needs to. Some things may require your joint attention for a longer period of time to thoroughly investigate. And some things he will be contented to study all by himself once he has seen them up close. If you keep yourself open to what his needs are you will be learning about what interests him and what to pursue further in order to satisfy his curiosity.

## What You Can Do to Help At Home

Children's far vision develops before their near vision. Since it is through seeing that your child learns best, give him every opportunity to put his thoughts and feelings into pictures. Like the kinesthetic child, the visual child will make great use of a large blackboard. It is a big space to draw picture after picture, to erase mistakes, and to use colorful chalks that make his drawings come to life. Crayons, water paints and finger paints, markers, colored papers, paste, and scissors—all of these things will delight your visual child. He will be an early scribbler and be concerned with staying in the lines of his coloring book as he gets older.

His room should be decorated with an eye for color. Babies respond more to bright primary colors than the pastels usually associated with them. When old enough, allow your child some input into decisions regarding his room. He has definite opinions about what appeals to him and what does not. This is the child who likes to have shelves for his books and toys and who enjoys arranging them in patterns.

Books will be early friends, especially those with bright, interesting illustrations. Even as a tiny baby, he will enjoy sitting on your lap looking in books and magazines or at things around the room. Crib toys and mobiles will enchant him. When you are outside, set him under a tree where he can watch the sun filtering through the leaves, or in a spot where he can see the cars as they drive by.

Dolls that can be dressed and undressed, a dollhouse (even one you can help make from books or blocks), and action figures to use for setting up scenes will give him hours of fun. He will enjoy playing alone or quietly with one friend, arranging figures in his "sets" to create a story, rather than inventing elaborate dialogues or noisy action.

Your visual child will go with you through art museums, zoos, stores, and neighborhood streets, examining everything carefully as you stroll along. When you come home from a trip or adventure, have him draw a picture about it. Then you can talk about it together. You will learn through his pictures what he felt and learned better than any words he could express.

On long rides you can play games of searching for particular objects, words, or colors. He will not be the child who is always asking "When will we get there?" He will be too busy watching what is passing by his window.

## Discipline

Make sure your visual child is looking at you when you are disciplining her. She will see from your face, more than from your words, that you are displeased. Oftentimes, a stern look from you is enough to stop her from continuing something you disapprove of.

Because too many words will be lost on the visual learner, keep lectures to a minimum; she simply does not take in all the words. Something else may catch her eye or she may daydream until you are finished. And do not ask for explanations of misbehavior; the visual child is rarely able to explain, if there was a reason in the first place.

## Rewards

For your visual child, a big smile from you is frequently all she needs for reinforcement. But any message at all will mean more if you make eye contact first. She will look for the expression on your face to support the words. If you praise her but show worry, anger, or frustration in your eyes, it will only confuse your visual child who hears the words but reads your face as well. As hard as it may be sometimes to separate yourself from your own concerns, it will make a great difference to your child if you can show her honest pleasure and pride while you are dealing with her.

When she starts scribbling and drawing, put her creations up for all to see. When she brings finished assignments home from school, make time for her to show you what she did right. She will not always *tell* you how she did, but when she knows you have *seen* her accomplishments, she will be satisfied.

When your visual child shows you her artwork, a specific compliment will show her you have really noticed: "What a great purple monster!"

This is the child for whom a chart for behavior modification will be most helpful. If you are trying to help him do the chores you expect from him around the house, make a weekly chart and a list of the duties under each day. Give him a shiny star for each chore finished. Those stars will give your visual child a real sense of accomplishment and help him learn how to organize his time later in life. Also, it is helpful to give him chores that have strong visual results. Dusting is not as visually rewarding in itself as sorting and folding a big stack of clothes into neat piles.

Another form of reward for a job well done is to promise a shared activity of your child's choosing when the task is completed. You might draw a picture together, play a board game, read a favorite book, or go to the library for a new book; but make sure the time is uninterrupted by outside calls or duties. This will help emphasize that this is *her* reward for a positive behavior.

In areas of interaction such as rewards, discipline, and interpreting emotions, it might be helpful to compare the responses you gave yourself on the "Parent Checklist" and those you marked for your child. Even if you are not a visual learner, you will need to study your child's face and actions as clues to how well he is doing. If he is angry or upset he may turn his face away, or even leave the room. He is not comfortable coming right out and telling you what is wrong, and he usually will not strike out or show any obvious physical reaction.

**Visual children may not tell you what is wrong, but you can tell what they are feeling just by looking at them.**

When he needs encouragement, remember he needs more than just a few words or a quick pat on the back. He is looking for you to notice what he is doing. If he needs your assistance to complete a project or task, it will be most helpful for him if you describe each step in sequence *as he does it*. A nonstop explanation from beginning to end will only be lost on him; he will not remember anything past the first or second step. Allow him the time to do the job himself, although many times it would be easier to step in and do it yourself. For visual learners, their apparent slowness in doing things is not a sign of inability. They check out every detail and angle before and after they actually do something. Structuring tasks to meet their needs and allowing time for them to work at their own pace will make an enormous difference in the achievement and confidence of visual learners.

## At School

Talk to your child's teacher about what you have observed. Very likely, she, too, will have noticed that your child likes to "see" things in writing or pictures to learn them. If you find that your child is having trouble with a particular subject, try to find out how it is being taught. Perhaps she cannot see the concept and needs help to visualize it. Perhaps where she is studying is too visually chaotic for her. Keep her teacher informed of any problems you detect, and ask her how you can help to reinforce her teaching at home.

## The Point of Intervention

The point of intervention, as discussed earlier, is when a child has not learned material as initially presented. For a visual child, this occurs when the teacher relies on auditory or kinesthetic strategies. The intervention must depend on visual models for the child to follow. In this way she can use her strength for learning and support even if the lesson is primarily in another modality. When she can see a visual example, she can translate that into her own action or her own speech. Keep *your* eyes open for difficulty with school subjects and try to find ways to help your child visualize concepts on which she needs extra work.

## Reading

Your visual child should have no trouble learning to read. Reading is primarily visual—*looking* at a word and understanding it. You can help your child get started at home by providing books filled with colorful illustrations for him to practice associating pictures with words. Let him choose a supply of books regularly from your local library.

Helping your child create picture stories will also strengthen his visual perceptions. Have him tell you the story in words and write those words under the appropriate pictures he has drawn. He will begin to associate the words with the pictures.

There are several good books for parents on helping their

children learn to read. Highlights for Children's *Growing Up Reading* by Linda Leonard Lamme (Acropolis, 1985) contains many useful suggestions for making reading an important part of your family's life. Dr. Lamme suggests, for instance, "Reading aloud has an influence upon children's reading development, their feelings of warmth with regard to their families, their development of curiosity, their knowledge of literature, and their knowledge of information contained in the books that are read." Reading aloud is important for all learners, but it will be particularly pleasurable for visual learners who will want to look at the pictures and who will want to have you show them the word you are reading. Many of these children learn to read without being taught—for they learn from the cereal box, store, and road signs. Activities to strengthen your child's visual perceptions in reading and suggested book lists can be found on pp. 135-140 and 165-178.

**A visual child learns to read by making the connection between written words and pictures.**

When your child reaches school and is given a reading program, talk to his teacher and find out what kind of approach is being used. If the teaching strategy concentrates on phonics— either in the book, with the teacher, or both—your visual child may run into trouble, for he cannot relate purely auditory material to the words without a strong visual model. He may read perfectly well but not do well in phonics exercises. He should not be forced to learn reading through phonics, but rather be allowed to use visual imagery and a sight approach.

A teacher related a story about a little girl in her class who was very bright but simply was not learning to read. Michelle was tested for learning strengths and her results showed her to be primarily visual, with her auditory modality the weakest of all. In fact, noise and sounds were disruptive to Michelle when she needed to concentrate. Her reading program was principally phonetic, and the mismatch between the child's strength and the material was telling. The teacher began to work with Michelle in a spot where she could screen out as much auditory distraction as possible. The teacher would give Michelle picture cards and words to match, and quiet time to think about what she was seeing. The teacher rarely even spoke to her during this time. Over a period of weeks Michelle had basically brought herself up to a level with the rest of the class. Her parents commented that she had become like a sponge at home, looking at books and absorbing new words and concepts every day. Most important, now Michelle can help herself by making sure she studies without the distraction of a radio or record player or other auditory interruptions.

If you are called upon to work with your child on reading, use your understanding of her as a visual learner to give her the input she needs. Talk with her teacher to see what materials are available to you that will support the school program while building on your child's visual concepts.

## Handwriting

Your visual learner will probably delight in the appearance of her handwriting. She will like to copy the letters with you at home. You can help her practice by supplying her with a notebook whose lines and spacing are correct for her level of writing skill. Having her copy letters and complete words will strengthen her skills not only in handwriting but word recognition as well. She will be able to construct letters and words by looking at them written correctly on the page. You will not need to describe them verbally. Care must be taken to

**Writing letters to match the models is very important!**

provide the correct visual models. Different forms of letters such as *a* and *g* can be confusing to a visual learner.

Have a model of the manuscript basic strokes and the correct letter forms available when she begins to write. Do not pressure the preschool child to make the letters correctly. With a model, the visual child will likely want to make the correct letter forms earlier than other children.

**All manuscript letters are made up of these six basic strokes: left to right, top to bottom, backward circle, forward circle, slant right, slant left.**

## Arithmetic

Arithmetic, as we have said, is easy to adapt to modality-based instruction because so much of it depends upon simple memorization. Once the rules are mastered through visual strategies, your child should have little trouble applying them to more advanced mathematics if you can give him the opportunity to perform the adding, subtracting, multiplying, and dividing visually.

Help him work through a problem by showing him the entire process before you explain. He will understand better what you are saying if he can see what the end result should be. In other words, if you are helping him learn to divide 63 by 3, write out the entire problem, *then* discuss it from beginning to end. He will *see* the process as a total picture in his mind.

*Growing Up Learning*

Practice with flash cards will also be beneficial for your visual learner, although he will not need to associate physical movement from the unlearned pile to the learned one. He will visualize the fact on each flash card and *see* it in his mind when he needs to recall it. You can also help him construct flash cards with problems on them to aid his visual memory of the processes involved.

## Spelling

*Seeing* correctly spelled words and studying them is the visual learner's best way to learn spelling. You can help her learn her spelling list by pointing out the sequence of letters in each word, drawing shapes around each word to emphasize how it is formed, and pointing out visual similarities and differences between words. You will find your visual child eventually writing a word to see if it *looks* right. She will never be able to do as well in a spelling bee as she does in a written test. The only way she can succeed orally is to have a clear picture of the words in her mind to "see" as she says the letters.

Sometimes the visual speller jumbles the letters in the middle of a word, interchanging letters such as *e, o,* and *a.* She seldom misses the beginning and ending letters of the word, or gives it the wrong number of letters. If you are helping your child memorize the spelling list, have her write the words out after looking at the list. Don't mark or circle words she has misspelled. That will only draw her attention to the wrong way to write the word. Write the word correctly next to the misspelled version, so she can see how it is spelled and compare the two.

## Lifetime Study Habits

If you help your visual child understand how to use her visual learning skills as a child, she will be able to learn each new concept that comes her way. She will know that writing things down reinforces them for her. She may not even refer back to her notes because having once seen it in writing, it is imprinted in her mind. Your visual learner should take copious notes during a lecture, for instance. Seeing in writing what the professor has said is vital to her learning.

**Organization, neatness, and quiet work habits signal the visual learner.**

When she is studying, show her how to organize her notes into a study chart or outline in which information is listed under important categories. During an exam she will see that chart in her mind. Highlighting with a marker in textbooks she owns will imprint that information in her mind. Again, when she is asked a question or tested on the material she will see the page and highlighted information.

Especially when it comes to kinesthetic and auditory tasks, visual children and adults will use visual strategies to master new skills. Brian is a bright, visual boy who wanted to learn how to play soccer. It was not a game that came naturally to him and he worked very hard learning how to play. When he started playing in actual games, he would look over to the sidelines to his father or coach to see what to do. He would pick up on an expression or a gesture that would tell him to be more aggressive or to try a certain play. He would not hear directions anyone would shout; a look was enough for him to know what to do.

For your visual child, the strategies he learns to help him in reading, writing, arithmetic, and spelling will be useful to him as he approaches new situations throughout life. Do not worry if he is not as verbal as another child nor as adept physically. He is a gifted observer and when he is ready to speak and to do, he does so with confidence and assurance in himself.

*Chapter 7*

# Your Mixed Modality Child

"Ann is not a terribly active child. She didn't start walking on her own until recently. She will play quite happily in her playroom, looking at books and toys, one by one, and delighting in shaking and studying any toy that makes noise. She is quick to hear the door when one of us comes home and calls to us to play dolls or to color with her. She loves to use every color crayon in the box."

—Parent of a fifteen-month-old

"Becky is extremely active. She doesn't like to sit still for anything with the possible exception of reading books with me. She turns the pages and will stop the story just to look at a favorite illustration an extra minute. Otherwise she's on the go from the minute she wakes up until she falls asleep. It's amazing how much she notices when she's outside. A bird on the grass, a plane way up in the air, a weed or wildflower in the park—she's fascinated by every detail and always runs over to investigate whatever catches her eye."

—Parent of a three-year-old

"Jason is a real dynamo! When he is outside and starts pretending, he grabs a stick to be a sword and declares what character he is and who I am to play.

Then he runs to find the `bad guys'! I have to act as lookout and tell him where to run to next—behind a bush or a fence, next to a wall, under the picnic table. Then he climbs his favorite tree and makes all sorts of rocket noises pretending to take off and fly and crash."

—Parent of a five-year-old

"David is a fairly active boy. When he was a toddler, his favorite activity was sitting on my lap, listening to a tape or record and following along in the accompanying picture book. But as soon as the story was over he'd be up and off to push his trucks or build a tower. Now that he's in school he enjoys all his subjects and gets good grades. He seems to learn everything so easily, it makes me wonder sometimes why he doesn't get all A's."

—Parent of a ten-year-old

Each of these children cannot clearly be classified in any one learning modality. They are equally comfortable in two or even three modalities. Ann is visual/auditory, Becky is visual/kinesthetic, Jason is auditory/kinesthetic, and David is a combination of all three. They are said to have mixed modalities.

## Mixed Modalities

All people are, of course, a combination of all three modalities. At different times in our lives and under different circumstances, each of us will use one specific modality more than another. In the sense that we use a combination of visual, auditory, and kinesthetic modes as a way of receiving information, everyone can be said to have mixed modalities. But most people have a dominant mode to which they will turn, especially under stress. And just as most people have a dominant mode, most people also have a secondary mode. The individual who has more than one dominant modality, or who uses the three modalities almost equally, is truly the person with mixed modalities. On the modality checklist, if the scores of the first two modalities are within five points of each other, that person has a mixed modality strength with the third modality being the weaker one. If all three modalities are within ten points of one another, all three are comparatively strong.

To illustrate, Table 3 shows the modality scores of the children described at the beginning of the chapter.

| Table 3 | Visual | Auditory | Kinesthetic |
|---------|--------|----------|-------------|
| Ann     | 38     | 38       | 24          |
| Becky   | 42     | 19       | 39          |
| Jason   | 27     | 39       | 34          |
| David   | 37     | 33       | 30          |

**In the classroom, visual and auditory modalities are called upon most often.**

A person with mixed modalities is able to shift comfortably between two or three modalities depending upon how the material is presented. Under stress, it is likely that she will revert to whichever of the two modes is most appropriate for the situation. Some adults may appear to have mixed modalities when actually they have a dominant mode and a secondary mode which, through training or experience, they have learned to use equally well. Under stress such an individual will still revert to his dominant mode.

Some adults with mixed modalities frequently are

displaying the effects of environmental influences, or their own adaptations in which they have learned how to use their dominant modality to such a degree that they are able to function in the other two areas without even being aware that they are doing so. One study of teachers tested for modality strengths found that 40 percent of them had mixed modalities, a high figure which might be explained by the fact that they learned how to use their different modalities, they had done well in school, and the success in going to school attracted them to teaching as a profession.

## The Child with a Mixed Modality Strength

As many as one-third of all children may have mixed modalities. The child with mixed modalities may be a combination of any two or all three of the modes we are considering, but most often she will be a visual/auditory combination. The child who is labeled "gifted" is frequently found to be the one with mixed visual and auditory modalities. This is no doubt true because of the great demands placed on the visual and auditory modalities, particularly in the elementary grades. When she is visual/kinesthetic or auditory/kinesthetic she will function more like a child with a single dominant mode because most of the formal learning that takes place, particularly that provided in school, is presented through the visual or auditory modes.

## The Visual/Auditory Learner

The visual/auditory learner is more talkative than the purely visual one, but better able to respond to visual input than the auditory learner. She may become so engrossed in a book that you won't hear from her for hours, but she also loves to get into discussions and debates when she's in the mood. In her spare time she is more likely to write, draw, or watch TV, possibly with the radio or stereo on at the same time.

Your visual/auditory child will have an easier time in school than many children since the material and teaching strategies call on her strengths. It may be most helpful for her to have a book or outline to refer to when a teacher's presentation is oral. When reviewing a lesson she may talk about what she has learned as well as use notes as support. She may be a good creative writer since she enjoys language and the written word. She knows what sounds good to her ear and she can put it on paper.

The only trouble you may have is getting her to *do* things. Taking action is probably her weak spot, since she is able to placate others with her words, or she is easily distracted. If your visual/auditory child is reading and you ask her to set the table, she may very well answer in the affirmative. But if she doesn't get up right away she will read on and on, unaware of how much time has passed since she said yes. If you ask her to put away some stuff in the attic she may carry one box and sit down to pore over old pictures. Once you have given her a task, you might check her progress occasionally to keep her on track.

## The Auditory/Kinesthetic Learner

The auditory/kinesthetic combination of mixed modes appears to be one that presents more problems. In a classroom situation demanding quiet and stillness, the auditory/kinesthetic child is always at a disadvantage. She is rarely allowed to use her strengths. The very things she wants to do to get involved in learning are the things that get her into trouble. You and her teacher should work together to find ways of tailoring her strengths to the classroom. The more she can subvocalize instead of talking and shouting, the less she will disrupt the class. Play whispering games with her to show how she can control her auditory expression. Find ways of using her kinesthetic energy constructively in class. If something needs to be written on the chalkboard, her teacher can ask her to do it. If papers need to be handed out, she is the one to ask. Giving her opportunities to move around throughout the day will make it easier for her to sit and concentrate when necessary.

Outside the classroom, other people may consider your auditory/kinesthetic child too boisterous. Unlike the visual/kinesthetic child, his "acting out" involves noise. If he is in a school chorus where he has to stand still in a group, he will cause trouble. It is inevitable that someone near him will get pushed, stepped on, or poked. But put him in a marching band and he will excel. He is the song-and-dance man, the stage actor, the one who moves well and has strong vocal expression as well.

**Being able to bang on an instrument—moving and making noise—delights the auditory/kinesthetic child.**

I know of a four-year-old, Jonathan, whose parents are involved with a community theater group. He spends his evenings at the theater while the group rehearses the next musical or comedy production. He never seemed to pay much attention to the rehearsal, he was always running up and down the aisles or playing with his toys. But one evening, during a break, Jonathan climbed up on stage and performed one of the music numbers, complete with choreography. Everyone in the theater stopped to watch him as he went through at least half the number perfectly. Without any apparent effort he had taken in every word, every step. More and more, as rehearsals for a play get closer to opening night, Jonathan points out things the adults forget, "Daddy, you are supposed to say this . . ." and "No, Mommy, you're supposed to go over there now."

Jonathan may find himself in trouble when he starts school, but if he can find his niche, he will do well. One auditory/kinesthetic person who succeeded academically and found his career strength is my dentist. He hums and whistles the whole time he is working on his patients. He does a good job carrying a tune and doing the refined physical movements required in his profession.

## The Visual/Kinesthetic Learner

The visual/kinesthetic person may find the classroom situation confining but his energy is at least quieter than the auditory/kinesthetic child's. It may well be that the visual/kinesthetic child can channel that energy more into small muscle movement and thus avoid getting into trouble quite so much. He will doodle and draw and carve in his desk. It may not be what the teacher likes, but it is less obvious and disruptive than noise. In fact, the visual/kinesthetic person is a real artist. He has a sharp eye and the physical ability to produce. A teacher would be wise to ask for the visual/kinesthetic learner's help when it comes to setting up displays, decorating for a seasonal holiday, or making posters for the bulletin board.

**A big sheet of paper and colorful crayons will let a visual/kinesthetic learner use his strengths to full advantage.**

One mother recognized her boy as clearly visual/kinesthetic. She told a story about a time he went to visit his grandfather and was allowed to borrow an old motorcycle. He needed a pouch to carry extra plugs and tools with him so he found a piece of leather and just started cutting away and

**Matching mental images with the appropriate movement is the special skill of visual/kinesthetic learners.**

sewing it together. He had no pattern to go by, but he knew what it would look like and he could carry out the image he had in his mind. This boy also loved wood carving. Again, he never made a mark on the wood, he knew what he wanted the finished product to look like and just where to cut to get what he wanted.

Visual/kinesthetic learners also do well in many sports. Their eye-hand coordination is well-developed. Catching a ball and throwing a ball accurately takes both physical ability and a good eye. In archery, riflery, tennis, volleyball, and many other activities, it is the skilled eye together with the refined kinesthetic movement that makes the difference between hitting or missing the right spot.

## The Visual/Auditory/Kinesthetic Learner

The child with three fairly equal modalities seems able to learn easily. Regardless of the methods used, she seems able to shift into the required mode and acquire what is being taught. When speaking with parents I have frequently said that if you could choose the modality of your own child, which I do not believe is possible, you should choose mixed, for then your role as a parent would be much easier. The child with mixed modalities tends to listen, watch, and receive, is able to speak her ideas with relative ease and, perhaps to a lesser degree, learns by doing. When she enters school, she learns to read regardless of the methods being used. As a matter of fact, the child with mixed modalities is the one who tends to "mess up" all educational research. During the time when the sight word approach to teaching reading was in vogue, the child with mixed modalities learned well. As a sounding or phonetic approach took over, the child with mixed modalities learned this way as well. As a matter of fact, I like to tell teachers that the child with mixed modalities learns even if we as teachers forget to come to school.

The child with mixed modalities is appreciated by her parents and teachers, often to the detriment of another child

**Some children learn no matter what approach is used. They can shift into whatever modality the situation demands.**

who has a single dominant mode. On the other hand, however, the child with mixed modalities may actually fail to learn how to learn or to question so that she fully understands. This may be a problem later on, but it makes the task at hand appear easier for she is generally able to complete it with a minimum of difficulty. The very evenness of her abilities makes her appear more cooperative and may result in adults presuming that she has higher ability than she actually does.

By high school age, the child with mixed modalities is less favored than in the earlier grades. The specific demands to acquire information at the high school level, often by teachers with a single dominant mode, will often allow individuals who

**Students may do especially well in a class where they share the same dominant modality as the teacher.**

share that same single dominant mode to perform outstandingly in a particular class. The child with mixed modalities, who was previously recognized for his abilities, must now depend upon what he has learned earlier and, if he has failed to learn how to study or to learn the fundamentals, he may have difficulty in maintaining a position of superiority.

Another important factor to consider when thinking of the child with mixed modalities is that it appears as though high-level creative performance comes only in the area of the dominant modality. It may be that the child with mixed modalities, because he has never been called to use a single mode at the very highest level, will have greater difficulty dealing with information in a creative manner rather than merely repeating it back or dealing with it in the manner in which it was taught.

## How You Can Help

For your child with two or three strong modalities, you can refer to the previous chapters and to the material in Part III for activities, games, and books that will appeal to him or her in particular. Try some of the strategies for a specific modality strength and see how much your child responds to them. Depending on the skill or concept involved, one modality may work better than another for your child, and by trying different approaches you will be able to determine what works best.

Many of the games and activities in Part III already combine two or three modalities—jumping rope while saying rhymes, scavenger hunts, using colored markers to draw from oral directions. As you look through the pages you will probably recognize the things that will be the most fun for your child. The games are always a success with groups of children because there are elements that appeal to each modality, allowing all children to use their strengths in all their diversity. Now that you are more familiar with the modality concept, watch a group of children at play and consider their behaviors. In a game of scavenger hunt, is there a child who runs all over the place in the hopes of passing near the spots where objects are hidden? Does one child repeatedly call out the names of the things he is looking for? Which child actually spots the objects first? You will not only learn about your own child, but about his or her friends and how they work together.

The ultimate goal, of course, is for everyone to integrate

**Playing together gives children the opportunity to discover and share each other's strengths.**

his modalities to as high a degree as possible. Those who are unable to shift from one mode to another learn to compensate by using their dominant mode.

*Chapter 8*

# Playing with Your Child

Playing is one of the most important ways children learn. It can be a relaxing, fun time you share with your child. It will also help show you your child's strengths, and help your child know his or her own abilities.

The following provides a sample of games and toys that have proven to be traditional favorites among children. All are coded to indicate modality preference. When a letter *K, A,* or *V* is printed in bold, it indicates a special appeal for that learning style. But do not let that limit your choices. Children love games of every variety, and sometimes a skill they have never tried before will be the most fun. Most games are made up of elements of two or even all three modalities and so hold interest for all types of learners. In a game of charades, for example, the kinesthetic person will love to perform, the visual person will watch intently to get clues to the answer, and the auditory person will shout out every option that comes into his head and talk over every guess with his teammates.

Children adapt games to their own modality strengths as well. Even sedentary games such as cards can be fun for kinesthetic learners who will slap down cards with extra energy and shuffle their stacks and drop the cards and pick them up and rearrange them, and so on. (In general, though, the smaller the movement the less interesting it will be to kinesthetic learners until they are older.) Auditory children like craft projects, and will make delightful objects while talking to themselves—which materials and which colors to use, how to put it together, what it

**Trying out different activities teaches children about themselves. They learn what they do well and how to use their strengths to help them.**

will look like, and where to put it. Then they will describe it to everyone they see after it's finished.

Naturally, some games do appeal to kinesthetic learners, some to visual, and some to auditory. Some children will do better in certain games from the very first, like the child who holds a ball and throws it perfectly on the first try. Other children need to develop the skills required to play ball, but almost all children want to learn to throw and catch and will learn no matter what their modality strengths. By exposing children to all sorts of activities you help them recognize their strengths and develop those strengths so that they can use them to help their weak areas.

## Games

The games described below are generally listed in order of difficulty. Those in the beginning are for younger children; those toward the end are for older children. Most games can be structured for the age of the child—short and easy when young, increasingly longer and more challenging as he or she gets older. If your child is not interested in a game or seems frustrated by it, stop playing. Games are meant to be fun, not stressful. You might try it again in a few weeks or months if the child is simply too young for it, or abandon it completely if it doesn't match your child's interests.

*Ball Games* **KV**

Playing any ball game will help develop your child's coordination and he will enjoy almost all of them, from simple games of catch to baseball, soccer, basketball, football, and volleyball.

**These children don't care about eye-hand coordination. They just know they're having fun!**

Start your young child with catching and throwing a large, light ball like a beach ball. Then move to smaller balls. Begin with short distances and move to longer ones, as the child becomes more proficient. Ball games build eye-hand coordination, as well as develop large and small muscle coordination. A Ping-Pong ball is fun for a child to throw and chase, and it makes sounds as it bounces!

In any game, remember your child's learning strength as you begin to play. For instance, tennis is a game enjoyed by many children and adults. For a visual child, a book on tennis might be helpful for her to see how to hold the racquet, how to swing, where to stand. Let your child watch as you demonstrate the motions. For an auditory child, talk about how to play and let her ask questions. Give her verbal cues on where the racquet should be, when to swing, and so on. For the kinesthetic child, start out by guiding her through the motions. Hold her hand, swing her arm with her. And when you start practicing, keep talk to a minimum, let her just play at her own pace.

*Obstacle Course*                                                      **K**

Create a simple obstacle course for your child to crawl, run, or

**Over, under, around, and through—the bigger the challenge the better!**

jump through by arranging chairs, boxes, hoops, and whatever you can think of, around a room or yard. Let the child figure out how to overcome each object until she reaches the end of the course.

### Rolling, Somersaults, Gymnastics         **K**

A patch of grass, padded carpet area, or mat is all you need. Let your child roll from side to side or down a hill or in a straight line. Have her stretch her arms above her head when she rolls. If she likes a mental image, tell her to think of herself as a log rolling.

Somersaults on grass, mat, or in water are a kinesthetic activity your child will delight in. Show her how to tuck her head under as she squats on the ground, then flip her body over in a tucked position. She should work up to doing a series of somersaults in a row.

There are endless possibilities for "gymnastic" activities with your child. A board (12 inches wide for young children down to 4 inches wide for older children) raised slightly off the ground can be a balance beam. Small objects, sturdy stools, or boxes can be "vaulted" onto, off of, and over. Jumping on two feet, hopping on one foot, going forward, going backward along a specified length with arms held up in the air or out at shoulder height are all good exercises for developing body awareness and coordination.

### Angels in the Snow         **K**

Play this game in the snow if you live in a cold climate, or in the sand where it is warm. Have the child lie on his back with arms and legs outstretched. Then he moves his arms up and down and his legs back and forth to form the impression in the snow or sand of an "angel" with wings and a skirt. When he stands up, he will see the angel he has made by involving his entire body. You can compare the sizes and shapes of the angels that every member of your family makes.

### Copycat Sounds         **A**

Have your child turn his back. Make different sounds and have him guess what they are, after he has tried to duplicate them. Or both of you close your eyes and listen to the sounds in the room or outside, and discuss what you hear.

*Follow the Leader*                                    **KVA**
Let one person be the leader. (Guess who always wants to be the leader and is the best leader, too!) The others line up in back of him and copy everything he does as quickly as possible. Run, jump, skip, clap, wave arms—whatever action the leader makes, the followers copy. The game can also include making sounds with the actions, announcing each action with a word, or making whoops and other sound effects.

*Mirrors*                                              **KV**
Two players stand facing each other, almost touching. (If there is one adult and one child playing, the adult should kneel to be more in line with the child.) One player is designated the leader

**"Can you do exactly as I do?"**

and moves in various ways—nodding, shaking, cocking her head to one side, raising and lowering arms, shrugging, bending to one side and the other, and so forth. The other player mirrors the leader's actions as closely as possible. It is easier for younger children to stay in one spot when mirroring, but older children might like to slide along the floor, turn around, try increasingly challenging actions to be mirrored. After a designated time, let players switch roles as leader and follower, or switch players.

*Simon Says* **AK**
Restless children have been entertained by this game for a long time. An auditory child will excel in it. You start out as leader and have your child stand and listen to your commands. Whenever you say, "Simon says do this," and make a movement of some sort, the child is to follow exactly. If you just say, "Do this," he should not move. If he does, he is disqualified. If he doesn't move, continue making commands until he forgets and follows one that is not prefaced by "Simon says."

*Memory* **V**
Arrange a number of objects of all sorts on a tray. Let the child study the tray for several minutes, then take it away. Have the child recite to you or write on a piece of paper every object she can remember. If you are playing with several children, the child who remembers the most objects wins.

*Guess What's Missing* **V**
Have your visual child study a particular room or a group of objects as used in "Memory." Then ask him to hide his eyes. Take away one object. Ask him to look again and identify the missing object.

*I Spy* **VA**
This game will get you through many long waits with a child. It can be played with two or more people. One person spots an object in the room and tells what color it is. The others must look around the room, identifying every object of that color until they guess the right one. The person who guesses correctly then spots the next object.

*Sightseeing*                                                          **V**

Before you go on a car ride, give your child a list of objects to look for during the ride. Depending on the age of the child, the list can be made up of hand-drawn pictures, pictures from a magazine, or written words. Have him check off each object on the list as he spots it. If more than one child is along, the first one who finds all the objects, or who finds the most by the end of the ride, wins. You can also play this game in a museum, at the grocery store, at the library, or almost anywhere you go.

*Puzzles*                                                             **VK**

Cut out a picture from a magazine and paste it on a piece of cardboard. Let dry and cut it into puzzle pieces. Have your child help you make the puzzle if he can. Then he may put it together.

**"Plink! Plink! Plonk. Whoops, this one needs some tuning!"**

*Water Glass Song*                                                    **AK**

Fill a number of glasses with water at differing levels. Let your child use a spoon to tap out familiar tunes or make up new ones. Be sure to use sturdy glasses, and watch the child so glass and water don't go flying.

*Telephone* **A**

This is a great game to play while waiting to be served in a restaurant. It keeps everyone occupied quietly. Have one person think of a sentence and whisper it in the ear of the person next to him. Then that person whispers it to the next one until it has circled the table. The last person says out loud what he heard. Everyone will be amazed at how the original statement has changed in its passage around the table.

*Round Robin Stories* **A**

Have one person start a story and others, in turn, add a portion to it. You can try this with poems, too. Each person will add a line to the poem.

*Hot and Cold* **VA**

Gather a group of children or family members for this game. Choose one person to be "it" and to leave the room while the rest of you hide a chosen object somewhere in the room. Call the person who is "it" back and have her search the room for the hidden object. The other players should hum. As she gets closer to the object, hum louder and louder, or say "hot," "hotter," "hottest." As she gets farther away, hum more softly, or say "cold," "colder," "coldest."

*Scavenger Hunt* **VK**

There are a number of varieties to this kind of game. You can play it with your child alone or make a group activity when several children are playing.

One way to play is to make a list of plants, animals, and objects you might find in your neighborhood, park, or just in your yard. Take your child on a nature walk and identify each item on your list. If you keep your list to small things (maple leaf, oak leaf, pinecone, rocks, feather, wildflowers, even flowering weeds) this can be a good start to a nature collection.

Another option is to hide things around your house or yard, give the children bags and then let them find the items. For younger children, you may hide things like peanuts, small bags of popcorn, snacks, fruit, or eggs, and see who can find the most. For older children, you can give them a list of things to find. You can also hide letter cards and have children find the letters in their name. This is a game that can be tailored to almost any age group, interest, and location. Just use your imagination!

**"I see one!" "I've got one!" "Mommy, they're finding all of them!"**

### Hide-and-Seek                                                     VK
One person is "it" and counts to a specified number while the others hide. The person who is "it" counts at a designated spot called "base." When she has finished counting, she shouts, "Ready or not, here I come!" and goes off to search for the other players. When she spots a player, she must tag him before he reaches the safety of base. The first person tagged becomes "it" on the next round.

### Sardines                                                          VK
A variation of hide-and-seek is "Sardines." In this game, one person hides while the others count. When the count is complete, the players all search for the person who is "it." As they find her, they quietly hide with her, scrunching in with her. The last person to find the "sardines" is "it" in the next round.

## Ghost in the Graveyard                                    VK

This is a good "cooling down" game. One person is the "ghost." The others lie on their backs or stomachs as quietly as they can. The ghost watches all the players carefully. If she spots anyone moving, she taps that person. The last person to be tapped wins and becomes the ghost in the next round.

## Marco Polo                                                AK

In a pool or on dry land choose one person to be "it." This person closes his eyes and counts to ten. The rest scatter as far as they can until he shouts, "Ready or not, here I come." Then, with eyes still closed, he begins calling, "Marco." The others, who are now standing in place, must respond by saying "Polo." On the basis of the sounds of their voices, the player who is "it" must find the other players and tag them. The last player tagged becomes "it."

## Hopscotch                                                  K

The old-fashioned game of hopscotch is a great reinforcer of numbers. Draw the hopscotch grid with chalk on pavement or a stick in the sand. A player throws a stone, stick, or small object into square 1, hopping over the square with the object in it, through the entire course from 1 to home (one foot in each single square, both feet in the doubles), turning around, and hopping back to the beginning, picking up the stone when he reaches that square on his way back. He continues by throwing the stone into square 2 and on up to 9. If the stone misses a square, or if the player makes a wrong hop along the way, the next player gets a turn. The first player to complete this routine wins.

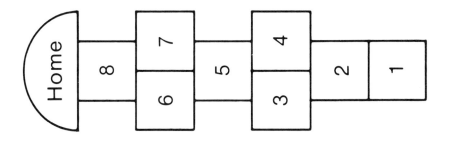

---

*Charades* **KAV**

Charades is played with two teams. Each team writes the names of books, movies, television programs, or songs on individual pieces of paper, enough for each player on the opposing team. With very young children you can use animal names. One player draws a piece of paper from the other team's pile and acts it out for his own team. Time how long it takes the team to guess the correct answer. Alternate turns until everyone has a chance to act out. The team with the lowest time score wins.

For an auditory child, provide words and have him act out rhyming words as clues. For example, rat—hat, cat, fat; had—sad, mad; took—book, cook; wall—fall, call, ball; heard—bird; fog—dog, hog; fun—sun, run; dug—tug, rug, bug.

"Is it a gorilla? Is it Frankenstein? I wonder what it is?"

*Jump Rope*                                                    **KA**

You need a long clothesline, a tree or pole to tie one end to, and
one person to turn the rope. It is much more difficult to learn to
jump and turn the rope at the same time, so start a child jumping
rope by having someone else turn while the child is mastering
the first "big jump, little jump" rhythms. Once she has the
rhythm, she can learn the jump rope chants and songs that add
another dimension to this activity.

*Taping*                                                        **A**

This is not so much a game as an open-ended activity for one,
two, or whole groups of children. With a tape recorder and blank
tapes your child's imagination is the limit. You can record Round
Robin stories described above; you can set up a pretend
television show with an interviewer and characters to be
interviewed. You can set up a situation from a favorite book,
movie, or television show—or make up new stories. Whatever
direction your child takes, listening to the recording will be as
much fun as making it.

*Buzz*                                                          **A**

This is an excellent game for practicing multiplication facts.
Choose one of the numbers your child is learning at school, for
example, three. Then you and your child, and/or other members
of the family, begin to count from 1 on. Every time you come to a
multiple of three or a number with a three in it, like thirteen (or
whatever number you have chosen), the player must say
"Buzz." If he forgets, he is disqualified.

*Other Games*

The above list is only a sampling of the traditional favorites
enjoyed by children for years. By playing such games, children
learn how their minds and bodies relate, and they learn what
they can do best. If you want suggestions about more games, ask
other children. They are the true experts. Ideally, see if you can
find a child whose learning strength matches your child's. Other
kinesthetic, auditory, or visual children will have discovered
what appeals most to them.

## Party Ideas with Games and Crafts

The games described below are grouped by theme. They can be used for birthday parties, informal groups, or used singly to liven up an ordinary afternoon.

### Circus Party

*Invitations*

Fold pieces of white paper in half to make folders. Cut circles of different colors to represent balloons. Glue three balloons to the front of each folder. Decorate as shown. Write your invitations inside. Include the time of the party and your name and address.

*Decorations*

Make a balloon clown to put at each place at the table. Put a few small wrapped candies and a tiny favor (plastic animal, envelope of gummed stars, and so on) into a balloon, blow it up, and tie the end. Draw a face on the balloon with markers. Cut a pair of feet from cardboard. Make a small hole in the center and a slit at the back, as shown. Poke the end of the balloon through the hole, twist and stretch the end of the balloon, and bring it up and insert it into the slit.

*Centerpiece*

Make a circus train from empty cereal boxes. Cover the locomotive with colored paper. Add a tiny box to the top. Draw pictures for the sides of the animal cages. Cover the narrow sides with colored paper. Cut the wheels from cardboard and glue them in place.

*Kiss the Clown Game*

Draw a large clown on cardboard (perhaps the side of a large grocery carton). Cut it out and color it or decorate with cut paper. Cut a hole for the mouth. Blow up a small red balloon and tie the end. Insert the end through a hole where the clown's nose should be. Glue the clown to the side of a small grocery carton.

Mark a line about five feet from the clown. Standing behind the line, the guests take turns throwing candy kisses in the clown's mouth. Whoever "kisses" the clown most often is the winner.

## Game of Skill

Place a muffin pan on the floor. Tape a piece of cardboard to one edge of the pan to form a ramp. Put a piece of wrapped candy into each of the muffin cups. Mark a starting line about five feet in front of the ramp. Each player gets a turn to roll three small balls at the muffin cups. If the ball goes into a cup, the player gets that piece of candy. Replace the candies as they are won.

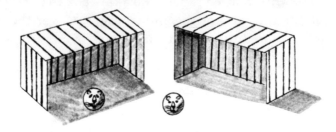

## Lion in the Cage

Cut away one long side from each of two shoe boxes to make the cages. Place them so that the cutaway side is at the bottom. Draw bars on the other sides. Draw lion faces on two Ping-Pong balls. Two players at a time start at a line about ten feet in front of the cages. On hands and knees, each tries to blow his lion into his cage first—no hands.

## Acrobat's Delight

Set up a course consisting of a series of obstacles, each with a sign attached telling the players what to do, for example, a pillow on the floor with the sign "Turn somersault here," a straight chair tipped over to make a tunnel with a sign "Crawl through." Every player who completes the course is a winner.

*Balloon Volleyball*

Divide the players into two teams. Give each team member a balloon of the same color. One team gets all yellow balloons, for example; the other team, all red ones. Tie a string across the room about as high as the average player's head.

Teams line up on opposite sides of the string, and each player tries to throw his balloon over the string and have it touch the floor on the opponent's side. The other team is doing the same, at the same time trying to bat the opposing team's balloons back over the string. Every time a red balloon touches the floor on yellow's side of the string, the red team gets one point. The first team to score twenty points wins.

## Snowman Party

*Invitations*

Draw snowman invitations on folded paper (making sure one side touches the fold). Cut out and color. Write your invitations inside.

*Decorations*

Make a fluffy snowman decoration. Roll a newspaper tightly and secure with rubber bands. Put glue over all of the roll except the bottom. Cover with cotton balls, adding a second layer where you want the snowman to be fatter. Cut hat, scarf, and features from colored paper and glue in place.

Cut snowman-shaped place mats from large pieces of white paper. Decorate with crayons or markers.

*Refreshments*

• Hot Appple Drink. Heat four cups of apple juice in a saucepan, adding a dash of cinnamon just before pouring into mugs. Makes four servings.

• Ice-Cream Snowballs. For each serving, put two scoops of vanilla ice cream in a bowl and sprinkle with shredded coconut.

• Snowman Snacks. Spread round crackers with soft cream cheese. Make features with raisins.

*Fox and Geese*

Mark a large circle, with four straight paths to the center and a center space, by tramping lines in the snow. Or use chalk if you are playing on bare pavement or masking tape if you are indoors. Choose one player to be the fox, who stands in the center. Other players (the geese) run around the circle and up and down the paths, trying to stay out of the reach of the fox. Fox chases them, also running only on the circle and paths. Each "goose" caught is placed in the center. The last one caught becomes the fox for the next game.

*Draw a Snowman*

Give each player a sheet of paper and a pencil or crayon. At a signal, each person begins to draw a snowman—behind his back. Whoever does the funniest drawing is the winner.

## Snowballs

Number six plastic-foam balls from 1 to 6. Each guest takes a turn at pitching them into a basket. Add up the numbers on the balls that land in the basket to obtain each score. The highest score is the winner.

## Glove Scramble

Turn the gloves and mittens of your guests inside out. Place them in a pile in the middle of the floor. At a signal everyone scrambles for his own gloves in the pile. The first person to have his gloves on right side out wins.

## Topsy-Turvy Party

*Invitations*

Write invitations on paper plates. Use a different colored pencil or felt-tipped marker for each word. Print some letters upside down or backward. Briefly describe your party—when and where it's to be—and ask everyone to dress in topsy-turvy style.

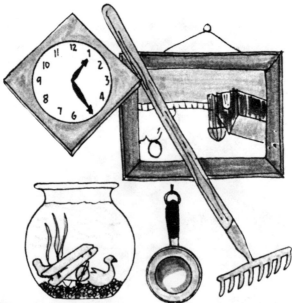

*Decorations*

Any confusion you create will help give your party the jumbled atmosphere you need for decoration. For example, bring in things that don't ordinarily belong in a living room or family room—pots, pans, and other kitchen utensils; gardening tools; and so on. Hang pictures upside down; set clocks ahead and calendars to another month.

Empty fishbowls make imaginative decorations. Fill them with water and objects that don't belong in water, such as plastic or glass animals, birds, and airplanes. When you begin decorating, you'll discover there's an endless variety of things you can do to create amusing confusion. But remember, when the party's over, there'll be the inevitable cleanup time, so decorations should be practical, too, for easy tidying up.

*Daffy Drawings Game*
Give everyone paper and crayons or markers to draw a scene or object, putting in something that's out of place—a man walking a bird on a leash, a square-wheeled automobile. Allow ten minutes for this. Then award a prize for the cleverest idea.

*Costume Capers*
Form a circle into which everyone steps, in turn, to display his or her costume. Shoes on the wrong feet, mismatched socks, clothing backward or wrong side out, are a few things your friends can wear to look topsy-turvy. Vote for the most ingenious outfit.

## No Laughing

Players form a straight line or a circle. One person has to know the game beforehand and act as the leader. That person starts by saying "I am going on a hike and I am going to take . . ." Then he names some object such as "a paper bag." The next person repeats the sentence but substitutes an object of his own, which might be "a peanut-butter sandwich." This goes on until everyone in the group has had a turn.

Then the leader repeats his sentence, "I am going on a trip and I am going to take a paper bag," adding "because I might want to fill it with pinecones I find along the way." Now the second player must repeat the sentence, substituting the item he had mentioned earlier. His sentence would be: "I am going on a hike and I am going to take a peanut-butter sandwich because I might want to fill it with pinecones I find along the way."

No matter how silly some of the sentences may sound, no one must laugh or smile. Anyone who does so is out of the game.

When it's the leader's turn again, he might add, "And then I am going to burn it in the campfire tonight." The others would then repeat their sentences as before.

## Off and On Game

A blanket is placed on the floor. At your command, the players are supposed to jump "on the blanket" and "off the blanket" several times, until confused by the repetition "off the blanket, off the blanket," when those who jump *on* are out. Keep playing until you have a winner.

Then try the same game topsy-turvy style. "Off" means "on" and "on" means "off."

*Z to A*
Just for fun, see how many of the guests can recite the alphabet backward. Who can do it fastest?

## Toys

The following suggestions are listed in appropriate age categories and by modality strength. It is important to remember, however, that children use toys in ways that fit their own strengths, so that almost any toy can be fun for a child. A tape recorder is a delight to an auditory child, but the aspect of punching buttons, stopping and starting, ejecting the tape and pushing it back again is fun for the kinesthetic child, as is dancing or pounding an instrument in time to the music when it is actually playing. Many toys listed under one column or another are universally enjoyed by all children; and placement in a particular column indicates which modality will be developed primarily. When you are buying a toy for your child, you will want to keep his or her modality in mind, but only as a guide, not as a limitation.

# Infants and Toddlers

*Kinesthetic*
mobiles that
  move when hit
  or grasped
cradle gym
rattles with
  interesting
  shapes or
  textures
nesting toys
stacking rings
bench with large
  pegs and
  hammer
foam or plastic
  balls
large blocks
push or pull toys
four-wheeled
  riding toys
sandbox, shovel,
  pail
large cars, trucks

*Auditory*
crib music box
stuffed animals
  with music
  boxes or squeaky
  noises
cradle gym with
  bells and other
  sounds
rattles
push or pull toys
  with sounds
bowls, pots,
  wooden spoons

*Visual*
crib mobile
stuffed animals
  with bright
  colors, definite
  features
cradle gym
clutch balls
unbreakable
  mirror
colorful blocks
stacking toys
simple puzzles

## Two to Five-Year-Olds

### Kinesthetic
climbing dome
building blocks
construction sets
dolls, action
  figures, puppets
modeling clay
crayons, paints,
  finger paints,
  large paper
chalkboard, chalk
blunt scissors,
  paste
lacing toys
soft wood,
  hammer, nails
train sets
sandbox, shovels
rocking horse,
  broomstick
  horse
tricycle
punching bags

### Auditory
play telephone
  (commercially
  made, or two
  cans with string,
  or section of old
  rubber hose)
music box
musical jack-in-
  the-box
bells, toy musical
  instruments
  (kazoo,
  xylophones,
  drums,
  tambourine,
  cymbals)
dolls, action
  figures, puppets
child's record
  player, tape
  recorder, records
  and tapes

### Visual
sorting toys
stringing toys
crayons, paints,
  coloring books
dolls, dollhouse,
  action figures
farm, village,
  community
  playsets
chalkboard, chalk
kaleidoscope
child's magnifying
  glass
puzzles
sewing cards
Viewmasters,
  filmstrip

# Six to Ten-Year-Olds

*Kinesthetic*
bicycle
skates (roller or
  ice)
jump rope
pogo stick
construction sets
model sets
weaving looms
chemistry set
table top sports
  games
ball and bat, ball
  and racquet
jacks
marbles
robots

*Auditory*
blank tapes and
  tape recorder
musical
  instrument
board games
  involving
  questions and
  answers
puppet theater
computer games
  with vivid sound
  effects

*Visual*
child's camera
telescope
microscope
jigsaw puzzles
paper dolls
craft sets
pencil and paper
  puzzles
board games
clothes for "dress
  up"
computer games

*Chapter 9*

# Developing Basic Skills

Activities that help your child develop basic skills can be as enjoyable as playing games if you keep modality strengths in mind. By providing activities that use your child's learning strength you can challenge her to grow and give her the success that will encourage her to attack new skills and problems.

The activities included here will show what your child excels in and enjoys. You can then provide additional materials that match your child's needs and interests. A librarian, preschool teacher, or elementary teacher will be able to suggest other sources; or you can consult one of the excellent children's catalogues such as Constructive Playthings (U.S. Toy Co., 1985-1986) which offers books and basic skill materials as well as toys. Any published material will be a source for modality-specific activities once you know how visual, auditory, and kinesthetic strengths are utilized.

## Reading Readiness

*Left-to-Right Progression*

For all children, start with large movement and work toward increasingly smaller movement when working on left-to-right progression. Kinesthetic children can move large objects from their left to their right side, make whole arm movements from left to right, and work down to finger movement left to right across a page. Visual children can look at an object on the left side of a room and slowly look over to an object on the right. Eventually work from far vision to near vision until children can follow lines across a page. For auditory children, have them say "left to right" as they make a left-to-right movement with their bodies or eyes. Occasionally when you read to your child, show that you begin at the left and go to the right. When your child begins to print, encourage him to begin at the left. Use the following example to pattern activities at home. You may provide drawings of your own or post magazine and catalogue pictures on either side of a bulletin board.

Left to Right
Move your finger on the line from the bird to the nest. Then move your finger from left to right to show where all the others go.

*Visual Discrimination*
Visual discrimination is developed by observing likenesses and differences, matching familiar objects, basic shapes, and eventually letter forms and words. For a kinesthetic child, you may start by providing pairs of real objects to pick up and match

(for example, fruits, hand tools, blocks of different sizes and shapes, writing instruments). Eventually you can put four or five pairs of plastic letters on the table for the child to match. When matching objects on a printed page, let the kinesthetic child move her finger from one object to another, or match by drawing lines with a crayon or pencil. For auditory children, help them develop visual discrimination by talking about the objects and their different characteristics. When matching letters and words, have your auditory child say the letters or words aloud to help him discriminate the differences. Visual children may enjoy using different crayons to color matching pairs.

Matching Fruit
Look at each piece of fruit at the left.
Find the piece of fruit like it at the right.

# Matching
Look at each robot at the left.
Find the robot like it at the right.

# Matching Pictures

Look at this star.         Find the other star exactly like it.

Look at this wheel.        Find the other wheel exactly like it.

Look at this flower.       Find the other flower exactly like it.

## On Your Own With Words
Look at each thing in the first group.
Say the word below it.
Find the same thing in the second group,
and say the word below it.
Now find this word in the third group.

        ship

hat          ship        fence        bee

bee

        snowman

ship         hat

stamp        snowman                              hat

       fence

fence        bee         stamp        snowman     stamp

Karen    Robin    Undine    George

Look at each child's name.
Find below a picture of something
that begins with the same letter.

robot    giraffe    kangaroo    umbrella

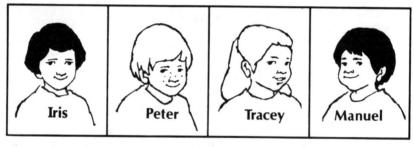

Iris    Peter    Tracey    Manuel

Look at each child's name.
Find below a picture of something
that begins with the same letter.

truck    mask    ice cream    piano

*Auditory Discrimination*

Auditory discrimination in visual children can be aided by the
use of picture cards, color cards, and letter cards. Some of the

activities below are useful because they give picture clues to rhyming words. The visual child can use the pictures and printed letters; the auditory child can say the words aloud. For kinesthetic children, interest in rhyming words can be increased by using action rhymes and finger plays where movement accompanies the rhyme. In an activity such as "Wrong Rhymes" below, have the kinesthetic child clap or make a specific movement when he hears a specific sound. At a wrong sound, he should not move. Also, for kinesthetic children, interest may be added to purely auditory or visual activities by providing a physical reward for correct answers. For example, each time a kinesthetic child can identify rhyming words or sounds that are different, let him get a block and build a tower. See how tall a tower he can build for right answers.

For each activity below, a few examples are given. If your child enjoys any particular activity, you may develop more on your own. The activities are taken from *Listening Games for Elementary Grades* by Margaret John Maxwell (Acropolis Books, 1981) and from *Getting Ready for Phonics,* and *Learning More about Phonics,* both compiled by Constance McAllister (Highlights for Children, Inc.).

### Double Trouble
Read each group of items. Child identifies the item which was mentioned twice in the group.

| | |
|---|---|
| 1. 5, **4,** 2, **4,** 1, 3 | 1. g, l, **o,** p, m, **o,** t |
| 2. 6, **8,** 3, 5, **8,** 2 | 2. s, **k,** a, m, e, t, **k** |
| 3. **9,** 6, 7, **9,** 2, 5 | 3. p, h, **u,** m, a, **u,** r |
| 4. 5, **6,** 1, 3, **6,** 9 | 4. **a,** n, y, e, **a,** p, s |
| 5. **5,** 9, 8, 4, 1, **5** | 5. m, i, **g,** h, n, u, **g** |

### Wrong Rhymes!
Read each group of words. The child identifies the word in the group that doesn't rhyme.

| | |
|---|---|
| 1. bug, rug, **sit,** tug, dug | 6. yet, bet, get, **sad,** let |
| 2. hat, **bag,** rat, cat, fat | 7. **sun,** sink, wink, mink, link |
| 3. but, nut, **dog,** hut, putt | 8. bin, pin, **hit,** tin, win |
| 4. rod, pod, sod, **hit,** cod | 9. pill, will, sill, **ball,** fill |
| 5. fun, run, **rat,** ton, bun | 10. sand, hand, band, land, **den** |

## Following Directions

Your child needs a red, blue, green, and black marker or crayon. Read each sentence. The child writes the required letter, numeral, or figure.

1. Write a blue 9 and a red S.
2. Write a green 3 and a black Q.
3. Write a red 2 and a blue F.
4. Write a black 0 and a green M.
5. Write a blue 7 and a black X.

1. Draw a blue circle and put a red dot in it.
2. Draw a green triangle and put a blue dot in it.
3. Draw a red square and put a green circle in it.
4. Draw a blue circle and put a red circle in it.
5. Draw a red square and put a green square in it.

## Rhyme Game 1

For each clue, say a word that rhymes with *shark*.

1. Noah kept his animals on an _____ .
2. Opposite of light.
3. "On your _____ , get set, go!"
4. Place to play in the city.
5. Dog-talk.

## Rhyme Game 2

For each clue, say a word that rhymes with *bear*.

1. What you breathe.
2. Rip.
3. Two shoes are a _____ .
4. Table and _____ .
5. It grows on your head.

## Rhyming Sandwiches

Make three "sandwiches" by putting together the kinds of foods that rhyme.

# Find a Rhyme

Look at each picture word
on this side of the page.

Find a word that rhymes with
it on this side of the page.

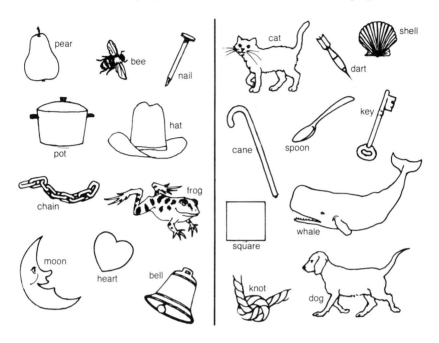

# Rhyming

Find a rhyme for each word in the list below.
The pictures will give you clues.

chin
mix
fig
house
hip
bill
rake
bit
star
crown

*Action Rhymes and Finger Plays*

Young children love the combination of rhyme and action. There are many old favorites known by preschool and kindergarten teachers. You may want to look through poetry books for young children and develop action to match some of the poems.

## Wiggle Fingers

### Wiggle fingers.
### Wiggle so.
(Wiggle fingers of both hands.)

### Wiggle high.
(Raise hands above head
while wiggling fingers.)

### Wiggle low.
(Lower hands
while wiggling fingers.)

### Wiggle left.
(Wiggle fingers on left hand.
Keep right hand still.)

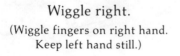

### Wiggle right.
(Wiggle fingers on right hand.
Keep left hand still.)

### Wiggle fingers out of sight.
(Move both hands behind back
while wiggling fingers.
Clasp hands behind back.)

*Growing Up Learning*

# Circus Time: An Action Rhyme

Being in the circus is a wish away.
Come with me and play today.

Walk the tightrope,

Be a clown,

Walk like an elephant and
turn around.

Jump a hoop . . .
and take a bow.

Circus time is over now.

## Tired and Sleepy—A Finger Play

Tired and sleepy, the thumb went to bed.
(Fold thumb down on palm.)

The pointer, so straight, fell down on his head.
(Fold index finger down on palm.)

The tall man said he would cuddle up tight.
(Fold middle finger down on palm.)

The ring finger curled himself out of sight.
(Fold ring finger down on palm.)

Last of all, weary and lonesome, too,
the little one hid, and he cried, "Boohoo."
(Fold little finger down on palm.)

## A Finger Play

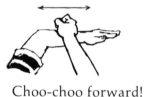

Here is the train.
(Make fist
with right hand.)

And here is the track.
(Hold left arm level.)

Choo-choo forward!
Choo-choo back!
(Place fist on arm,
move it
forward and back.)

Here are the wheels,
going clackety-clack.
(Rotate hands around
each other.)

Poof! goes the smoke from
the big smokestack!
(Move hands up quickly
in mushroom shape.)

## Puzzles, Headwork, and Creative Thinking

The following section provides material that will challenge children to think about the things they see, hear, and do. Some activities provide visual clues and illustrations for the visual child; some can be shared just in conversation; some imply movement for the kinesthetic child to do or remember doing. The questions posed are generally easier in the beginning of the section and become more difficult toward the end.

Questions are designed to get children thinking about relationships—cause and effect, outcomes, inferences, reality and fantasy—all of which are so important to reading comprehension. The questions do not have set answers. Each child will have his or her own answers. As you read through you will note there are groups of questions that relate to kinesthetic, auditory, and visual awareness. You might start by asking some questions in the area of your child's strength, but do not limit yourself to these. Getting your child to think about all of his or her modalities will increase self-awareness.

What's wrong in each of these pictures?

fish

pigeon

squirrel

frog

bear

Name things you can do that none of
these creatures can do.
What can each one do that you cannot do?
If each of these creatures had money, what
could he or she do with it?

Draw a line with your finger from each
creature to its home.

Which could you hide in your hand?

paper clip     scissors     penny     tablespoon     button
rabbit     bottle     stamp     apple

Which of these things grow shorter with use?

book   ruler   candle   scissors   eraser   crayon   fountain pen

Which of these could happen?
Which could not?

Which of these words can easily be pictured?

| owl | of | book | any |
|------|-------|--------|---------|
| boat | ax | the | box |
| that | was | lobster | thought |
| when | cube | dragon | easy |
| mind | tiger | snake | fox |
| car | for | with | and |
| but | think | this | chair |
| try | clown | much | donkey |

tiger

turkey

stool

chair

lion

Which of these have eyes?
Which have four legs?
Which have four legs and are living creatures?
Did you ever see a three-legged creature?
Did you ever see a four-legged creature
that could fly?

Which would you use to draw a straight line?
To mark a board for sawing it?
To measure the distance around
your chest or head?
To draw a circle?

The first pail is full of apples,
the second full of water, and
the third full of blocks.
Suppose you quickly turned
each pail upside down,
emptying it on a level sidewalk.
Which would scatter widest
on the sidewalk?
Which would be hardest to put
back in the pail?

Which children are old enough to do
some regular chores at home?
To feed themselves?
To put themselves to bed?
To bathe themselves?
To learn to cook a family meal?
To manage a regular allowance?
To sew a button on their clothes?
To do homework?
To walk six blocks to and from school?
To care faithfully for a pet?
To get themselves ready for school?

What Can You See?

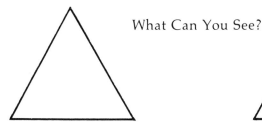

Anyone can see one
rectangle here.

Most boys and girls
can locate five triangles
in this drawing.

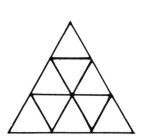

Now, can you locate
thirteen triangles here?

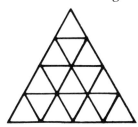

How many triangles
can you find here?

Can you put your elbow into your ear?

Is your heart above your knees or below your knees?

Name some jobs around the house that a girl or boy from six to twelve years old can do. What jobs do you do at home?

Which are harder, your teeth or your fingernails?

What is noisier when you eat it, a carrot or a piece of cheese?

If you wake up in the middle of the night, how can you know if it's raining?

What makes more noise, a baby playing or a baby asleep?

Can you say your name backwards?

How can you tell what a store sells before going inside?

Which might you notice first when you walk in a room—a new piece of furniture or a new book on a shelf?

Is the inside of an apple the same color as the outside? The inside of an orange the same as the outside? How about a watermelon?

Can you follow these directions? Put your hands together around both your legs and under your knees.

Why can you drink milk faster than a big dog can?

Does your upper jaw move when you chew? Does your lower jaw?

Could you peel a potato?

Which did you learn first, to throw a ball or to catch a ball?

Is a large dog always louder than a small one?

Which do you like better, the sounds a robin makes or the sounds a crow makes?

Try to say each of the following words in a way that matches the feeling—happy, angry, sad, scared, surprised.

Imagine waiting to go into a movie theater as other people who just saw the movie leave. How can you tell whether they liked the movie or not? Whether it was a funny movie or not?

Are the holes in a pepper shaker larger or smaller than the holes in a salt shaker? Why?

Could an elephant go through a door of your house?

"A new family moved into the house next door today," said Ruth. How could she have known this?

Did you ever fall down in the mud?

Can you stand on one foot?

Which is heavier, a baby or its father?

Which are easier to wash clean, the back of your hands or your fingernails?

Could your mother walk in your shoes? Could you walk in hers?

Does a toad hop the way you hop? Does a rabbit? Does a bird?

Could you carry water in a sieve?

Which did you learn to do first, sit alone or stand alone?

Which has the broader nail on it, your big toe or your thumb?

Can a cow crow? Can a dog moo?

"I must put some oil on the hinges of that door," said Mr. Marcus. Why did he say that?

How many animal sounds can you imitate?

Does steam come down from a teakettle or go up from it?

Which has larger wings, a fly or a butterfly?

Which is usually larger, a cup or a bowl?

One morning after a light snow Millie said, "Some rabbits have been running around in the yard." But Millie hadn't seen the rabbits. How did she know?

Do you take a bath with your clothes on?

Why do we have chairs?

Did you ever fall out of bed?

Would you like to ride an elephant?

How tall would you like to be?

Can you move your chin without using your hands?

Could you run as fast as another child can go on a tricycle? On a bicycle?

Which is easier, to count ten things lying together or to count ten bouncings of a ball?

Show how you can whisper.

Why do some clocks have alarms?

Does a bird sing when it is frightened?

Which is bigger, a bee or an ant?

Which is more, a drop of water or a spoonful of water?

How can you see the bottom of your feet?

*Growing Up Learning*

"We need to score. There is only one minute left in the game," said the coach. What sport might the team be playing?

What do you wear to go swimming? Sledding? Horseback riding?

Which will spill more easily when you carry it in a pail, water or sand?

If you wanted to carry two full glasses of water without spilling them, would it be easier to carry one in each hand or to put both glasses on a tray?

What sports usually do not have teams?

Name something you did that made you feel glad.

Did you ever see your heart? How do you know you have one?

Name some things you can stretch.

Which would make a sidewalk slippery to walk on: sand, wet soap, banana peels, oil, ice, dry cinders, soft mud?

The puppy was in the kitchen. Mother was in the living room. Several minutes passed and she heard no noise in the kitchen. "That puppy must be getting into mischief," she said. Why did she say this?

If your parents speak a foreign language, why would it be a good idea for you to learn this language from them?

Why do you suppose some musical instruments are called woodwinds? Can you name some?

Two men were in the woods on a pitch-dark night. One of them said, "An animal is running away from us." How did he know?

Fire trucks are often painted a bright color. Why is this?

Name something you saw that made you feel glad.

When a rubber ball bounces more than once, does it bounce higher on the first bounce or on the second?

Bob was looking at an apple tree in blossom. "There won't be many apples on that tree this year," he said. What caused him to say that?

Thunder and lightning take place at the same time. Why do we see the lightning before we hear the thunder?

Mrs. Martin looked out her window and saw children some distance away coming from the high school football game. "Our team must have won," she said. How could she have guessed that?

Is it easier to draw a car or a face? Why?

Name some things which go into the trash.

We usually pay before entering a movie theater. What other places require payment in advance?

Did you ever know a person who was older than his or her own aunt?

Name several kinds of animals that often live in houses with people.

## Tricks and Teasers

This section is generally for older children and provides challengers for children to try alone or tricks they can perform for others. For children who may show little motivation to read, try using these tricks to arouse their interest. Write a trick on a separate card and give it to a child. She must be able to read the card in order to do the trick for you. Being able to do a trick for parents and friends is great motivation for all children and you may soon find yourself providing many of these and looking for more!

● Have a piece of soap in your pocket for this trick. Have someone blindfold you, then have him pass a hat, asking each guest to drop in a coin. Someone then removes a coin, notes the value and date, and hands it to you. As you accept the coin, smear a bit of soap on it from your fingers. Drop the coin in the hat, shake it well. Using the other hand, find the soapy coin.

● Sew a penny securely in the corner of a handkerchief and have it ready in your pocket.

Borrow a penny from someone in the room. Let everyone examine it and note the date on the coin.

Pretend to wrap the penny in the handkerchief but actually keep it concealed in one hand. Tap the handkerchief on the table so the others will think the penny is wrapped inside. Let them feel the coin but do not allow the handkerchief to leave your hand.

Lay the handkerchief loosely on the table. Pick up a cup with the hand in which you are holding the borrowed coin. Pass the cup under the table directly under the handkerchief. Take a deep breath and blow on the handkerchief. At the same time let the coin drop from your hand into the cup. The clink of the coin will make it seem that the penny has passed through the table into the cup.

Shake the handkerchief to show there is nothing in it. Then bring the cup from under the table and show the coin about, calling attention to the date.


● Place on a table 15 small objects like toothpicks or buttons. Each player in turn picks up 1, 2, or 3 of them, whichever he pleases. The player to pick up the last object wins the game.

Here is the secret of winning. If there are 12, 8, or 4 objects left on the table and it is your opponent's turn, you can win, no matter how he plays. Suppose there are 12 when he is to play. If he takes 1, you take 3. If he takes 2, you take 2. If he takes 3, you take 1. In each case the number left will be 8 when it is his turn. In the same way the number of objects can be reduced from 8 to 4, and then he cannot possibly win.

Whenever it is your turn to start first, you can always take 3, leaving 12 for your opponent's first turn.

When he starts the game by taking either 1 or 2, you can bring it down to 12. But if he takes 3 at the beginning, you must try to leave 3 or 4 as soon as you can, or he may win.

Just remember the numbers 12, 8, and 4. The better you know the game and the faster you play, the longer it will take your opponent to learn the secret.


● Carefully pour water into a clean, dry glass until it is full. Do NOT spill any water on the outside of the glass. When everyone has decided the glass will hold no more water, ask them how many pennies can be dropped into the glass before the water will overflow. Then take one penny at a time and SLOWLY SLIDE it into the water, then drop it. Keep dropping pennies. Sometimes as many as twenty pennies can be added to the glass.

● The next time you want to mystify a friend, cut yourself in half with a piece of yarn. Sound next-to-impossible? With only minutes of practice, you can make the trick look possible.

Cut a piece of yarn about five feet long. Tie the ends together so you have a big loop of yarn. Hold the loop behind your back with your thumbs through the loop. Stretch your arms wide apart to pull the yarn tight. Then in seconds, you will be able to whisk the loop from the back of your waist to the front of your stomach. It will look as if you had slipped the yarn forward though your body.

Here's how: Bring your hands together in front of you. Slip the forefinger of your right hand into the loop beside your left thumb. Then quickly let your right thumb slip out of its end of the loop, and snap your hands apart until the yarn is pulled tightly across your stomach. Like magic, the yarn now will be stretched in front of you instead of behind you

Tips to make the trick look good: Hold the yarn in a straight line close to your body at both the beginning and the end of the trick. Point your hands downward, with your thumbs behind your fingers.

## Crafts

All children love craft projects. They love creating with their own hands, looking at it as it develops and displaying it when it's finished. They talk about it as they do it and when they show it off later. There are many excellent craft books available for children either through your library or local bookstore.

Envelope Puppet

Make a cut across the back of a business-size envelope one-third of the way down. Now seal the envelope above and below the cut.

Turn the envelope over. Draw a line across the front of the envelope at about the same level as the cut on the back. Above the line draw a face and hair. Below the line draw clothes for your puppet. Color as you like.

Or, instead of drawing the clothes and features, you may wish to cut them from yarn, cloth, or construction paper and glue in place.

Slide your three middle fingers into the cut in the back of the envelope. Your thumb and little finger make arms for your puppet.

## Saltbox Puppet

Cut off the top (about one inch) of a saltbox. Draw a face on the top.

Staple an 8-by-8-inch piece of fabric around the rim of the saltbox top. (You might have to pleat material to make it fit.) Stitch or staple the open seam together. Staple ribbon or lace around fabric edges.

Insert one hand into puppet and grasp edges of spout. Move the spout back and forth when puppet talks. Cradle the puppet's head in your other hand.

## Bat Branch

Cut two cups from an egg carton for each bat. Glue these to each side of wings cut from black paper. Cut pointed ears and glue in place. Use paper-punch dot eyes and a mouth cut from red paper. Glue a thread to each bat. Hang the bats from a branch.

Use colored yarn to hang the bat branch as a mobile.

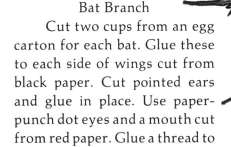

## Fabric-leaf Mobile

Glue a variety of colorful fabrics to both sides of several pieces of heavy paper. Cut leaf shapes from this. Tie a string on each leaf. Suspend the leaves from a small branch. Hang where the leaves will catch the breeze and flutter.

## Insect Nut Pictures

Draw or paint a background on a piece of cardboard. Glue half a walnut shell to the background to represent the body of an insect. Add legs and a head with markers or crayons.

## Modeling "Clay"

Combine in a bowl: 1 cup salt, 2 cups flour, 1 cup water, 3 tablespoons cooking oil. Mix well. Put on a floured board and knead.

Poke a hole in the ball of "clay" with your finger. Put several drops of food coloring into the hole. Knead again and watch it become colored. You may want to add a few drops of peppermint extract (or any favorite extract) for an interesting smell. Store in an airtight plastic container.

## Pictures with Rice

Draw a picture on heavy paper or cardboard. Instead of coloring it with crayons or paint, fill in each area with grains of rice in the color you want. To color the rice, fill a small jar half-full with raw rice. Add three or four drops of food coloring, and shake to distribute the color. Make purple by combining red and blue coloring, orange with red and yellow, and so on. When the coloring has dried, attach the rice by covering one area at a time with glue and sprinkling the rice over the glue. When dry, blow away any rice that has not stuck in place.

## Cotton-Ball Pictures

Pull several cotton balls into petal shapes. Glue them around a cotton-ball center. Add a pipe-cleaner stem and cotton-ball leaves.

Paint with tempera. (For an unusual effect, apply small dabs of paint on the petals.)

Use cotton balls to make other things like butterflies and bugs. Add details with a felt-tipped marker.

**Children will find what they like in a book and turn to it often.**

## Books For Your Child

Kinesthetic children start out loving books they can touch and feel—books with pictures that pop up and have things to do. They grow to enjoy adventure stories and anything filled with action. They may also appreciate many areas of nonfiction such as sports, science, biographies, and histories written with a sense of what people were *doing*. Auditory children start out loving books with rhymes and rhythms, word plays, and poetry. Later, they enjoy books with plenty of dialogue and a sense of the flow and sound of language. Visual children start out loving books with colorful, vivid illustrations and grow into stories with detailed descriptions of characters, places, appearances.

The following is a brief list offering suggestions for books to read with your child. The code at the end of each entry stands for Kinesthetic, Auditory, Visual. A letter printed in bold indicates a special appeal for that learning style. But do not let this limit your selection. Children will react to different books in a variety of ways and will find what they enjoy in each. For example, the reason Dr. Seuss books are so popular is that they have strong elements for each learning style. The illustrations are imaginative and humorous; the language is full of rhyme and nonsense sounds; the characters are always full of action.

Some of the books listed are wordless. The strong illustrations will appeal to the visual learner, but the development of a story in one's own words—whether by parent or child—is marvelous for the auditory learner. The wordless books are listed in the preschool section but can be enjoyed equally by older children as their language abilities increase.

The age divisions are also meant as a guide, not a boundary. Some young children who have developed a love for books will look and listen to a slightly longer book, while some older children just being introduced to books will enjoy the shorter stories. Use your own judgment and your knowledge of your child's interests.

The author extends his thanks to the Montgomery County, Maryland, Public Libraries, Children's Services Department, for their assistance in compiling this list.

*Preschoolers*

Ahlberg, Janet and Allan. *Each Peach Pear Plum.* New York: Viking, 1979.                                                                       **V**

Ambrus, Victor. *Mishka.* New York: Warne, 1978.        **KAV**

Anno, Mitsumasa. *Anno's Alphabet: An Adventure in Imagination.* New York: Crowell, 1975.                                              **AV**

——. *Anno's Counting Book.* New York: Crowell, 1975. (wordless)                                                                              **AV**

——. *Topsy Turvies.* New York: Weatherhill, 1970.        **AV**

Arkin, Alan. *Tony's Hard Work Day.* New York: Harper, 1972. **K**

Asbjornsen, Peter C. and J.E. Moe. *Three Billy Goats Gruff.* New York: Harcourt, 1957.                                                          **A**

Bang, Molly. *Ten, Nine, Eight.* New York: Greenwillow, 1983. **A**

Barton, Byron. *Building a House.* New York: Greenwillow, 1981.                                                                               **K**

Bemelmans, Ludwig. *Madeline.* New York: Viking, 1960.        **A**

Boynton, Sandra. *A Is for Angry.* New York: Workman, 1983. **K**

Brown, Margaret Wise. *Country Noisy Book.* New York: Harper & Row, 1940.                                                                      **A**

——. *Goodnight Moon.* New York: Harper, 1947.              **AV**

——. *Nibble, Nibble.* Reading, Mass: Addison-Wesley, 1959 (Poetry).                                                                            **A**

Brenner, Barbara. *Snow Parade*. New York: Crown, 1984.    **V**

Bruna, Dick. *I Know about Shapes*. Los Angeles: Price, Stern, Sloan.    **KV**

Burningham, John. *John Burningham's ABC*. Indianapolis: Bobbs-Merrill, 1964.    **V**


Campbell, Rod. *Henry's Busy Day*. New York: Viking, 1984.    **K**

———. *Wheels*. New York: Harper & Row, 1985.    **K**

Carle, Eric. *The Very Hungry Caterpillar*. New York: Philomel, 1969.    **VK**

Chase, Richard. *Jack and the Three Sillies*. New York: Houghton Mifflin, 1950.    **A**

Ciardi, John. *Fast and Slow*. Boston: Houghton Mifflin, 1975.    **A**

Conklin, Gladys. *I Like Butterflies*. New York: Holiday House, 1960.    **K**

———. *We Like Bugs*. New York: Holiday House, 1962.    **K**

Crews, Donald. *Truck*. New York: Greenwillow Books, 1980.    **KV**

———. *Freight Train*. New York: Greenwillow Books, 1978.    **KV**


De Brunhoff, Jean. *Story of Babar, The Little Elephant*. New York: Random, 1933.    **V**

DePaola, Tomie. *Popcorn Book*. New York: Holiday House, 1978.    **KV**

DeRegniers, Beatrice Schenk. *It Does Not Say Meow*. New York: Seabury, 1972.    **A**

Dubanevich, Arlene, *Pigs in Hiding*. New York: Four Winds Press, 1983.    **V**

duBois, William Pene. *Lazy Tommy Pumpkinhead*. New York: Harper, 1966.    **V**


Emberley, Barbara. *Drummer Hoff*. Englewood Cliffs: Prentice-Hall, 1967.    **A**

Emberley, Ed. *Great Thumbprint Drawing Book*. Boston: Little, Brown, 1977.    **K**

*Ernie and Bert Can—Can You?* New York: Random House, 1982.    **K**

Ets, Marie Hall. *Play with Me*. New York: Viking, 1955.    **V**

Gag, Wanda. *Millions of Cats*. New York: Coward, 1928.     **A**

Galdone, Paul. *The Little Red Hen*. New York: Seabury, 1973.  **A**

Gillham, Bill. *Let's Look for Numbers*. Boston: Houghton Mifflin Co., 1975.     **V**

Goodall, John. *The Adventures of Paddy Pork*. New York: Harcourt, 1968. (wordless)     **KAV**


Harper, Wilhelmina. *The Gunniwolf*. New York: Dutton, 1967.     **A**

Hawkins, Colin and Jacqui Hawkins. *Pat the Cat*. Racine: Western, 1984.     **K**

Hill, Eric. *Where's Spot?* New York: Putnam. 1980.     **K**

Hoban, Russell. *A Baby Sister for Frances*. New York: Harper, 1964.     **A**

Hoban, Tana. *Count and See*. New York: Macmillan, 1975.     **V**

Hughes, Shirley. *Up and Up*. Englewood Cliffs: Prentice-Hall, 1979. (wordless)     **KAV**


Keats, Ezra Jack. *The Snowy Day*. New York: Viking, 1962.  **KV**

———. *The Trip*. New York: Greenwillow, 1978.     **KV**

———. *Whistle for Willie*. New York: Viking, 1964.     **KA**

Krauss, Ruth. *A Hole is To Dig*. New York: Harper, 1952.     **K**

Kunhardt, Dorothy. *Pat the Bunny*. Racine: Western, 1942.     **K**


Le Sieg, Theodore. *The Eye Book*. New York: Random House, 1968.     **V**

Lionni, Leo. *Swimmy*. New York: Pantheon, 1963.     **V**

*Little Green Caterpillar; One Green Frog; Wheels Go Round*. New York: Grosset & Dunlap, 1982. (All books with sturdy pages and circles cut out to poke fingers through.)     **K**

Livermore, Elaine. *Find the Cat*. Boston: Houghton Mifflin Co., 1973.     **V**


Mayer, Mercer. *A Boy, a Dog, and a Frog*. New York: Dial, 1967. (wordless)     **AV**

McCloskey, Robert. *Blueberries for Sal*. New York: Viking, 1948.     **V**

———. *Make Way for Ducklings*. New York: Viking, 1941.     **V**

Niland, Deborah. *ABC of Monsters.* New York: McGraw-Hill, 1976.  **K**

Perkins, Al. *The Ear Book.* New York: Random House, 1968.  **A**
——. *Hand, Hand, Fingers, Thumb.* New York: Random House, 1969.  **K**
Potter, Beatrix. *The Tale of Peter Rabbit.* New York: Warne, 1903.  **V**

Raskin, Ellen. *Nothing Ever Happens on My Block.* New York: Atheneum, 1966.  **K**
Robbins, Ken. *Tools.* New York: Four Winds Press, 1983.  **K**
Rockwell, Harlow. *I Did It.* New York: Macmillan, 1974.  **K**

Sandburg, Carl. *Wedding Procession of the Rag Doll.* San Diego: Harcourt Brace Jovanovich, 1967. (Poetry)  **A**
Scarry, Richard. *Richard Scarry's Best Word Book Ever.* New York: Western, 1963. (Also, *Richard Scarry's Busiest People Ever, Busytown Pop-up Book, Cars and Trucks and Things That Go, Color Book,* and others.)  **KV**
Sendak, Maurice. *In the Night Kitchen.* New York: Harper, 1970.  **KV**
——. *Where the Wild Things Are.* New York: Harper, 1963.  **KV**
Seuss, Dr. *Hop on Pop.* New York: Random House. (Also, *Green Eggs and Ham; One Fish, Two Fish, Red Fish, Blue Fish; The Shape of Me and Other Things; Horton Hatches the Egg,* and many others under Random House and Beginner Books.)  **KAV**
Smollin, Michael. *Alligator's Color Book.* New York: Random House, 1981.  **V**
Spier, Peter. *Crash! Bang! Boom!* New York: Doubleday, 1972.  **AV**
——. *Gobble, Growl, Grunt.* New York: Doubleday, 1971.  **AV**
——. *Noah's Ark.* New York: Doubleday, 1977 (wordless).  **AV**

Ward, Lynd. *The Silver Pony.* Boston: Houghton Mifflin, 1973. (wordless)  **AV**
Wells, Rosemary. *Max's Ride.* New York: Dial. 1979. (Also, *Max's New Suit, Max's First Word, Max's Toys.*)  **KV**

Wildsmith, Brian. *What the Moon Saw*. London: Oxford University Press, 1978. **V**

Witte, Eve and Pat Witte. *Touch Me Book*. New York: Western, 1961. **K**

Wright, Blanche. *The Real Mother Goose*. Chicago: Rand McNally, 1916, 1965. **A**

Yashima, Taro. *Umbrella*. New York: Viking, 1958. **A**

Zacharias, Thomas. *But Where Is the Green Parrot?* New York: Delacorte, 1968. **V**

Zemach, Harve. *Mommy, But Me a China Doll*. New York: Farrar, Straus & Giroux, 1975. **A**

---

*Five to Eight-Year-Olds*

Aardema, Verna. *Why Mosquitoes Buzz in People's Ears*. New York: Dial, 1975. **V**

Aesop. *Once in a Wood: Ten Tales from Aesop*. New York: Morrow, 1979. **V**

Alexander, Sue. *Small Plays for You and a Friend*. New York: Seabury, 1973. **K**

Allard, Harry. *Miss Nelson Is Missing*. Boston: Houghton Mifflin, 1977. **V**

———. *The Stupids Step Out*. Boston: Houghton Mifflin, 1974. **V**

Andersen, Hans Christian. *Princess and the Pea*. New York: Seabury Press, 1978. **V**

———. *The Ugly Duckling*. New York: Scribner, 1965. **K**

Ardizzone, Edward. *Little Tim and the Brave Sea Captain*. New York: Oxford, 1936, 1978. **A**

Arnosky, Jim. *Drawing Life in Motion*. New York: Lothrop, 1984. **KV**

Balian, Lorna. *The Aminal*. Nashville: Abingdon, 1972. **KAV**

Blegvad, Lenore, editor. *Hark! Hark! The Dogs Do Bark: And Other Rhymes About Dogs*. New York: Atheneum, 1976. **A**

Blegvad, Lenore and Erik. *The Great Hamster Hunt*. New York: Harcourt, 1969. **K**

Briggs, Raymond. *Jim and the Beanstalk*. New York: Coward, 1970. **V**

Broekel, Ray. *Police*. Chicago: Children's Press, 1981.  **K**

——. *Trains*. Chicago: Children's Press, 1981.  **K**

Brown, Marcia. *Stone Soup, An Old Tale*. New York: Scribner, 1947.  **V**

——. *Listen to a Shape*. New York: Watts, 1979. (Also, *Touch Will Tell, Walk With Your Eyes*.)  **KAV**

Brown, Marcia and Charles Perrault. *Cinderella*. New York: Scribner, 1954.  **V**


Carlisle, Norman and Madelyn Carlisle. *Bridges*. Chicago: Children's Press, 1983.  **K**

Carlson, Bernice. *Let's Pretend It Happened to You*. Nashville: Abingdon, 1973.  **K**

Carrick, Carol. *Sleep Out*. New York: Seabury, 1973 (Also, *Lost in the Storm, The Accident*, and others.)  **K**

Charlip, Remy, and Mary Beth. *Handtalk, An ABC of Finger Spelling and Sign Language*. New York: Four Winds, 1974.  **K**

Charlip, Remy, and Jerry Joyner. *Thirteen, Arm in Arm*. New York: Scholastic Book Services, 1975.  **K**


DePaola, Tomie. *Prince of the Dolomites*. New York: Harcourt, 1980.

——. *Strega Nona*. Englewood Cliffs: Prentice-Hall, 1975.  **V**

Devlin, Wende and Harry Devlin. *Cranberry Thanksgiving*. New York: Parents, 1971.  **K**


Fisher, Aileen. *I Stood Upon a Mountain*. New York: Thomas Y. Crowell, 1979.  **A**

——. *Out in the Dark and Daylight*. New York: Harper & Row, 1980.  **A**

Flora, James. *The Great Green Turkey Creek Monster*. New York: Atheneum, 1976.  **K**

*Fox Went Out on a Chilly Night*. An old song illustrated by Peter Spier. New York: Doubleday, 1961.  **AV**


Godden, Rumer. *The Old Woman Who Lived in a Vinegar Bottle*. New York: Viking, 1972.  **V**

Grimm, J.L.K. *Hansel and Gretel*. New York: Dial Press, 1980.  **V**

——. *Snow White and the Seven Dwarfs.* New York: Farrar, Straus & Giroux, 1972. **V**

Hoberman, Mary Ann. *A House is a House for Me.* New York: Viking, 1978. (Poetry) **A**

Hodges, Margaret. *St. George and the Dragon.* Boston: Little, Brown, 1984. **V**

Holman, Felice. *At the Top of My Voice and Other Poems.* New York: Scribner, 1970. **A**

Hutchins, Pat. *Don't Forget the Bacon.* New York: Greenwillow, 1976. **A**

Isadora, Rachel. *Ben's Trumpet.* New York: Morrow, 1979. **A**

Jeffers, Susan. *Hiawatha* (Henry Wadsworth Longfellow). New York: E. P. Dutton, 1983. **A**

Kennedy, Richard. *The Contest at Cowlick.* Boston: Little, Brown, 1975. **KA**

Krementz, Jill. *The Fun of Cooking.* New York: Knopf, 1985. **K**

——. *A Very Young Dancer,* New York: Knopf, 1976. (Also, *A Very Young Gymnast, A Very Young Skater, A Very Young Circus Flyer, A Very Young Rider.*) **K**

Kuskin, Karla. *Any Me I Want to Be.* New York: Harper & Row, 1972. **A**

——. *Dogs and Dragons, Trees and Dreams.* New York: Harper & Row, 1980. (Poetry) **A**

Langstaff, John. *Oh, A Hunting We Will Go.* New York: Atheneum, 1974. **A**

——. *Sweetly Sing the Donkey.* New York: Atheneum, 1976. **A**

Lewis, Claudia. *Up and Down the River: Boat Poems.* New York: Harper & Row, 1979. **A**

Livingston, Myra Cohn. *A Lollygag of Limericks.* New York: Atheneum, 1978. **A**

——. *O Sliver of Liver.* New York: Atheneum, 1979 (poetry). **A**

Lobel, Arnold. *Frog and Toad Are Friends.* New York: Harper, 1970. **V**

Marshall, James. *George and Martha*. Boston: Houghton Mifflin, 1972. **V**

Mayer, Mercer. *East of the Sun and West of the Moon*. New York: Scholastic (Four Winds), 1980. **KAV**

McCloskey, Robert. *Lentil*. New York: Viking, 1940. **A**

McCord, David. *Every Time I Climb a Tree*. Boston: Little, Brown & Co., 1967 (peotry). **A**

McDermott, Gerald. *Anansi, The Spider, A Tale from the Ashanti*. New York: Holt, Rinehart & Winston, 1972 **V**

McPhail, David. *Henry Bear's Park*. Boston: Little, Brown, 1976. **KV**

Merriam, Eve. *Bam! Zam! Boom!*. New York: Walker & Co.: 1972 (poetry). **A**

———. *It Doesn't Always Have to Rhyme*. New York: Atheneum, 1964. **A**

———. *There Is No Rhyme for Silver*. New York: Atheneum, 1962. **A**

Minarik, Else Holmelund. *No Fighting, No Biting!* New York: Harper, 1958, 1978. **K**

Moore, Lilian. *See My Lovely Poison Ivy*. New York: Atheneum, 1975 (poetry). **A**

Mosel, A. *Tikki Tikki Tembo*. New York: Holt, Rinehart & Winston, 1968. **A**

Oakley, Graham. *The Church Mouse*. New York: Atheneum, 1972. **V**

Parrish, Peggy. *Amelia Bedelia*. New York: Scholastic, 1970. **KAV**

Peet, Bill. *The Wingdingdilly*. Boston: Houghton Mifflin, 1970. (Also, *Big Bad Bruce, The Knats of Knotty Pine, The Caboose Who Got Loose, Fly Homer Fly*, and many others.) **AV**

Perrault, Charles. *Cinderella*. New York: Scribner, 1954. **V**

Peterson, David. *Submarines*. Chicago: Children's Press: 1984. **K**

Rey, H. A. *Curious George*. Boston: Houghton Mifflin, 1941. **K**

Schwartz, Alvin. *In a Dark, Dark Room*. New York: Harper & Row, 1984 (poetry). **A**

Schwartz, Delmore. *"I Am Cherry Alive," The Little Girl Sang.* New York: Harper & Row, 1979.　**A**

Segal, Lore. *Tell Me a Mitzi.* New York: Farrar, Straus & Giroux, 1970.　**V**

Silverstein, Shel. *A Light in The Attic.* New York: Harper & Row, 1981.　**A**

——. *Where the Sidewalk Ends.* New York: Harper & Row, 1974. **A**

Small, Ernest. *Baba Yaga.* Boston: Houghton Mifflin, 1966.　**V**

Steig, William. *Amos and Boris.* New York: Farrar, Straus & Giroux, 1971.　**A**

——. *The Amazing Bone.* New York: Farrar, Straus & Giroux, 1976.　**AV**

——. *Tiffky Doofky.* New York: Farrar, Straus & Giroux, 1978. **A**

Stevenson, James. *That Terrible Halloween Night.* New York: Greenwillow, 1980.　**K**

Van Allsburg, Chris. *Jumanji.* Boston: Houghton Mifflin, 1981.　**V**

Viorst, Judith. *Alexander and the Terrible, Horrible, No Good, Very Bad Day.* New York: Atheneum, 1972.　**KV**

——. *The Tenth Good Thing About Barney.* New York: Atheneum, 1971.　**V**

Waber, Bernard. *Lyle, Lyle, Crocodile.* Boston: Houghton Mifflin, 1965.　**A**

Wilson, Forrest. *What It Feels Like to Be a Building.* New York: Reinhold, 1968.　**K**

Withers, Carl. *A Rocket in my Pocket.* New York: Holt, Rinehart & Winston, 1978.　**A**

Zolotow, Charlotte. *William's Doll.* New York: Harper, 1972. **A**

---

*Nine-Year-Olds and Above*

Aliki. *The Many Lives of Benjamin Franklin.* Englewood Cliffs: Prentice-Hall, 1977.　**K**

Asimov, Isaac. *How Did We Find Out about Genesis.* New York: Walker & Company, 1983. (From a series of "How Did We Find Out about..." books including Antarctica, Black Holes, Comets, Dinosaurs, Earthquakes, Life in the Deep Sea, Outer Space, and Volcanoes.) **KV**

Atwater, Richard. *Mr. Popper's Penguins.* New York: Dell, 1978. **A**

Avi. *Captain Grey.* New York: Pantheon, 1977. **K**

——. *Emily Upham's Revenge.* New York: Pantheon, 1978. **K**

Babbit, Natalie. *The Search for Delicious.* New York: Avon, 1974. **A**

Blos, Joan. *A Gathering of Days: A New England Girl's Journal.* New York: Charles Scribner's Sons, 1979. **V**

Blume, Judy. *Tales of a Fourth Grade Nothing.* New York: Dutton, 1972. **A**

Brewton, Sara, et al, editors. *My Tang's Tungled and Other Ridiculous Situations.* New York: Harper & Row, 1973 (poems and tongue twisters). **A**

Brink, Carol. *Caddie Woodlawn.* New York: Macmillan, 1935, 1970, 1973. **K**

Burchard, Marshall. *Sports Hero: Pete Rose.* New York: Putnam, 1976. **K**

Burchard, S. H. *Sports Star: Chris Evert Lloyd.* New York: Harcourt Brace Jovanovich, 1976. **K**

Burnett, Frances Hodgson. *The Secret Garden.* Philadelphia: Lippincott, 1911, 1938, 1962. (Paperback: Dell, 1971). **V**

Burroughs, Edgar Rice. *Tarzan of the Apes.* New York: Watson-Guptill, 1972. **K**

Butterworth, Oliver. *The Enormous Egg.* New York: Dell, 1978. **A**

Cleary, Beverly. *The Mouse and the Motorcycle.* New York: Dell, 1980. **A**

Collier, James Lincoln and Christopher Collier. *My Brother Sam Is Dead.* New York: Four Winds, 1974. **V**

Cunningham, Julia. *Burnish Me Bright.* New York: Pantheon, 1970. **K**

Dahl, Roald. *The BFG*. New York: Farrar, Straus & Giroux, 1982.  **A**

———. *Charlie and the Chocolate Factory*. New York: Knopf, 1964.  **A**

———. *James and the Giant Peach*. New York: Knopf, 1961.  **A**

Dalgliesh, Alice. *The Courage of Sarah Noble*. New York: Charles Scribner's Sons, 1954.  **V**

Dank, Milton. *Albert Einstein*. New York: Franklin Watts, 1983.  **K**

DeJong, Meindert. *Wheel on the School*. New York: Harper & Row, 1954.  **A**

du Bois, William Pene. *The Twenty-One Balloons*. New York: Viking, 1947.  **KAV**

Dygard, Thomas. *Winning Kicker*. New York: Morrow, 1978.  **K**

Eager, Edward. *Half Magic*. San Diego: Harcourt Brace Jovanovich, 1954.  **A**

Farley, Walter. *The Black Stallion*. New York: Random House, 1944, 1977.  **V**

Fleischman, Paul. *The Half-A-Moon Inn*. New York: Harper and Row, 1980.  **K**

Fleischman, Sid. *By the Great Horn Spoon*. Boston: Little Brown, 1981.  **A**

———. *Humbug Mountain*. Boston: Little Brown, 1978.  **K**

Forbes, Esther. *Johnny Tremain*. Boston: Houghton Mifflin, 1943.  **V**

Fritz, Jean. *Can't You Make Them Behave, King George?* New York: Coward, McCann, 1977.  **K**

Gannett, Ruth. *My Father's Dragon*. New York: Random House, 1948.  **A**

Gardiner, John R. *Stone Fox*. New York: Harper & Row, 1980.  **A**

George, Jean C. *My Side of the Mountain*. New York: Dutton, 1975.  **A**

Grahame, Kenneth. *The Wind in the Willows*. New York: Charles Scribner's Sons, 1953.  **A**

Heide, Florence Parry. *The Shrinking of Treehorn*. Holiday House, 1971.  **KA**

Henry, Marguerite. *Misty of Chincoteague*. Chicago: Rand McNally, 1947. **V**

Hicks, Clifford. *Peter Potts*. New York: Avon, 1979. **KAV**

Howe, James. *Bunnicula: A Rabbit-Tale of Mystery*. New York: Atheneum, 1979. **A**

Hunter, Edith Fisher. *Child of the Silent Night*. Boston: Houghton Mifflin, 1963. **A**


Jarrel, Randall. *The Bat-Poet*. New York: Macmillan, 1964. **A**


Lawson, Robert. *Rabbit Hill*. New York: Viking, 1944. **A**

Levoy, Myron. *The Witch of Fourth Street*. New York: Harper, 1972. **AV**

Lewis, C.S. *The Lion, The Witch and The Wardrobe*. New York: Macmillan, 1961. **V**

Lipson, Shelley. *It's Basic. The ABC's of Computer Programming*. New York: Holt, Rinehart, 1982. **V**

Liss, Howard. *Strange But True Sports Stories*. New York: Random House, 1976. **K**


Mayer, Mercer. *Liza Lou and the Yeller Belly Swamp*. New York: Four Winds, 1976. **KA**

McCloskey, Robert. *Homer Price*. New York: Viking, 1943. **KV**

Miles, Bernard. *Robin Hood—Prince of Outlaws*. Chicago: Rand McNally, 1979. **KAV**

Milne, A.A. *Now We Are Six*. New York: Dutton, 1927 (Poetry). **A**

Monjo, F. N. *The Drinking Gourd*. New York: Harper & Row, 1970. **A**

Mowat, Farley. *Owls in the Family*. Boston: Little Brown, 1961. **A**


Norton, Mary. *Borrowers*. San Diego: Harcourt Brace Jovanovich, 1965. **A**

Norris, Gunilla. *A Time For Watching*. New York: Random House, 1969. **A**

Nostlinger, Christine. *Konrad*. New York: Avon, 1983. **A**

O'Brien, Robert. *Mrs. Frisby and the Rats of Nimh.* New York, Atheneum, 1971. **A**

O'Connor, Karen. *Sally Ride and the New Astronauts.* New York: Franklin Watts, 1983. **K**

O'Dell, Scott. *Sarah Bishop.* Boston: Houghton Mifflin, 1980. **V**

——. *Sing Down the Moon.* Boston: Houghton Mifflin, 1970. **KAV**

Paterson, Katherine. *Bridge to Terabithia.* New York: Crowell, 1977. **V**

——. *The Great Gilly Hopkins.* New York: Crowell, 1978. **V**

Pinkwater, Daniel. *Fat Men from Space.* New York: Dodd, Mead, 1977. **A**

Prelutsky, Jack. *Nightmares: Poems to Trouble Your Sleep.* New York: Greenwillow, 1976. **A**

Rawlings, Marjorie. *The Yearling.* New York: Scribner's, 1938. **V**

Robinson, Barbara. *Best Christmas Pageant Ever.* New York: Harper & Row, 1972. **A**

Sachs, Marilyn. *Matt's Mitt.* New York: Doubleday, 1975. **K**

Schwartz, Alvin. *The Cat's Elbow and Other Secret Languages.* New York: Farrar, Straus & Giroux, 1982.

Selden, George. *Cricket in Times Square.* New York: Dell, 1970. **A**

Simon, Seymour. *Paper Airplane Book.* New York: Viking, 1971.

Skurzynski, Gloria. *What Happened in Hamelin.* New York: Scholastic, 1979. **A**

Slater, Jim. *Grasshopper and the Unwise Owl.* New York: Holt, Rinehart & Winston, 1979. **KV**

Slote, Alfred. *Hang Tough, Paul Mather.* New York: Avon, 1975. **K**

Sperry, Armstrong. *Call It Courage.* New York: Macmillan, 1940. **K**

Starbird, Kaye. *The Covered Bridge House and Other Poems.* New York: Four Winds, 1979. **A**

Stearns, Pamela. *Into the Painted Bear Lair.* Boston: Houghton Mifflin, 1976. **A**

Steele, William O. *The Magic Amulet*. New York: Harcourt Brace
  Jovanovich, 1979. **V**
Steig, William. *Abel's Island*. New York: Bantam, 1981. **A**

Taylor, Mildred. *Roll of Thunder, Hear My Cry*. New York: Dial,
  1976. **A**
Tolkien, J.R.R. *The Hobbit*. Boston: Houghton Mifflin, 1938. **V**

Viorst, Judith. *If I Were in Charge of the World and Other Worries*. New
  York: Atheneum, 1981 (poetry). **A**

Walker, Lester. *Carpentry for Children*. New York: Overlook,
  1982. **K**
White, E.B. *Charlotte's Web*. New York: Harper & Row, 1952. **V**
——. *Stuart Little*. New York: Harper & Row, 1973. **V**
——. *The Trumpet of the Swan*. New York: Harper & Row,
  1970. **V**
White, Robb. *Fire Storm*. New York: Doubleday, 1979. **K**
Wilder, Laura Ingalls. *Little House on the Prairie*. New York: Harper
  & Row, various dates. **V**
Williams, Jay. *The Hero From Otherwhere*. New York: Archway,
  1980. **K**

Zhitkov, Boris. *How I Hunted the Little Fellows*. New York: Dodd,
  Mead, 1979. **K**

*Chapter 10*

# Your Child in School

Your child will spend as many hours in school as he or she spends with you. Just as it is important for you to understand how to teach your child at home, so you should understand how your child is being taught in school. It is up to both you and the teacher to build on your child's strengths once he or she enters school.

## Modality-Based Instruction

Many schools, teachers, and educational publishers are now making modality-based instruction a part of their program structure. Educators have varying interpretations of the identification and interaction of modalities which no doubt will be clarified in the coming years as research and classroom studies continue. But if you understand what is happening during the school hours now, you will be better equipped to work with the school and the teachers to ensure the best for your child.

In general terms, modality-based instruction follows this sequence: the teacher presents the lesson in the best possible manner, using the strategies and tools he knows best. If, after initial presentation, the teacher determines that one or more students have not learned or do not understand fully, then he needs to find another way to teach so that these students do understand. This is the point of intervention. The teacher recalls the modality strengths of the children he needs to reach and provides instruction for them, either in small groups or individually.

## Teachers' Modality Strengths

As adults, we structure our environment according to our modality. This is also true of teachers and their classrooms. Teachers teach the way they learn best. If a teacher is strongly influenced by a single modality, he will use that strength when presenting information. When a teacher is not reaching a particular student, it is not because he is a poor teacher or the student is a poor learner. The solution is to direct instruction to that child's learning strength.

Let's take a look at three different classrooms and see how different modality strengths are evident.

Room 113, The Auditory Classroom: The physical organization of this classroom is not immediately noticeable. Teacher and student desks are grouped together toward the front and center of the room. The chalkboard is at the opposite end of the room from the teacher's desk. There is one bulletin board in the room with a seasonal display on it. Two learning centers and a listening station are along one side of the classroom.

The listening station has a tape recorder and a record player. There are numerous tapes and records that provide

**A listening station, tapes, records, and cassette recorders help meet the needs of auditory learners.**

instruction in basic skills, plus some records of sounds and music. Each of the learning centers has a cassette recorder in plain sight. The directions for each center are on cassette tapes.

Instruction in this classroom is mainly in the form of verbal discussion and lecture. Student talk is encouraged, and language lessons are accompanied by much discussion. Reading aloud is stressed. Reading instruction is built on phonics lessons. There are frequent spelling bees. The children are encouraged to do verbal math problems and games, and respond orally to flash cards. There is a constant "buzz" of activity as students chat back and forth about their lessons and other activities.

**An auditory teacher is likely to encourage group problem solving, giving students a chance to exchange ideas and opinions.**

Room 114, The Kinesthetic Classroom: The physical organization in this classroom is not evident at all. The teacher's desk is out of the way in the far corner. Items on the desk are in disarray; the desk is used mainly as a readily accessible storage space for blocks, beads, jar lids, scissors, and other assorted items. The student desks are lined up with wide aisles between rows. The center of the room is open space. Beyond the open space is the chalkboard. The chalkboard is used constantly. The open shelf space contains many items such as blocks, counters, models, diagrams, and construction materials. The shelves are organized by activities: art supplies, books, models, student-made materials. Around the room are many examples of student-made art pieces, including macrame, string art, and car and airplane models. The bulletin board is near the teacher's desk and contains geometric drawings by the children.

**Much physical activity distinguishes the kinesthetic classroom, where chalkboards and art supplies are always in use.**

Much instruction takes place in the open space in the center of the room. Acting out a scene or activity occurs frequently. The teacher provides guidance for fine motor tasks. Instructional examples are accompanied by models and gestures. The children are encouraged to write spelling words, either at their desks or on the chalkboard. Unknown words are traced. Children use their crayons frequently.

Room 115, The Visual Classroom: The physical organization in this classroom is immediately clear. The student desks are organized neatly in groups facing the teacher's desk. There are several bulletin boards about the room, each colorfully decorated and displaying material relating to some element of the current lessons. There are three learning centers identified by attention-getting artwork. The math center contains numerous graphs and pictures of math examples.

Posters, signs, and pictures are displayed everywhere about the room. The letters of the alphabet are in orderly display along the wall opposite the windows.

Much instruction takes place from the teacher's desk. Workbooks, worksheets, and pictorial presentations dominate instruction. Reading is frequently done silently, stressing a sight word approach. Configuration and pictures are used as clues for unlocking new words. Math drill is either from worksheets or flash cards. Spelling is practiced through the use of flash cards. Instructions to the children are often in the form of task cards or printed materials. Art activities are common, usually two-dimensional, with line, color, and shape stressed. Slide films and movies are often viewed to provide instruction or as a special activity.

## A Visit to a Classroom

Now let us observe one teacher's instructional strategy during a spelling lesson. The teacher is aware of her own modality strength and teaches from that strength, but she knows the strengths of her students and allows them to use their strengths to help them learn.

Ms. Cullen, a third grade teacher, is in the middle of a spelling lesson. Her strength is in the visual modality and she uses a visual method of teaching spelling. She is aware, however, that her modality strength is not shared by every student in the class and has adapted her lesson somewhat to accommodate the variety of modality strengths exhibited by her students.

The first student in her class to notice our arrival is Kit, an auditory learner. Even though we try to slip into the room quietly, Kit turns in her chair to find out who has come into the class.

The teacher is standing at the chalkboard pointing at each letter of the word written on the board. She addresses the class, "This is our first word. Look how it starts with a maximum letter, has two minimum letters in the middle, and ends with a maximum letter."

**Sounding out the letters helps the auditory child learn new words and recognize familiar ones.**

Kit, in the meantime, has picked up her pencil and taps her desk each time Ms. Cullen points to a letter. As the teacher points to the letters that constitute the word, Kit is sounding them out to herself "el, o, u, duh."

Ms. Cullen draws a line around the word to accentuate its configuration. Kit winces when the chalk makes a screeching sound as it is drawn across the board. While the teacher discusses the shape of the word, Kit continues to repeat to herself the sequence of sounds in the word. She is listening to herself, not the teacher, as she puts the sounds together to form the word *loud.*

"*Loud,*" she says to herself. "It means very noisy. I like to make all kinds of sounds. I guess I must be loud. But we're supposed to be quiet in class, except when we get to read aloud. Loud!"

While these thoughts are going through Kit's mind, the teacher has finished describing the configuration of the word. She turns to the class and says, "Who knows what this word means? How about you, Kit? You're a good speller. Tell us what letters are in this word and what it means."

Kit hesitates for a moment while looking at the word on the board. She is confirming that she has all the sounds right. Then she says confidently, "*L-o-u-d. Loud.* It means noisy."

The teacher smiles and replies, "That's right, Kit. You are

*Growing Up Learning*

such a good speller." Ms. Cullen knows that Kit is an auditory learner, and does not insist that she use the configuration cues. Ms. Cullen also realizes that the hesitation Kit showed before she spoke was not a sign that she did not know the answer, but indicated that Kit was transferring the letters from the visual display on the board to a series of sounds that she said to herself. Not only can Kit learn through the auditory modality, she can transfer cues from other modalities into the auditory.

As the teacher begins the next word in the lesson, we shift our attention to Hanley. During our visit, aside from a glance around the room, she has remained very still. Her eyes are glued to the chalkboard.

"Our second word is different from the first. It starts with a maximum letter, then has four minimum letters. The word is *brown,* and it is a color." Hanley looks at the letters, *b-r-o-w-n.* She closes her eyes for a moment, opens them, and looks at the word again. She takes her pencil and writes the word on her paper. "No," she says to herself, "that doesn't look right. I know the first letter is right, and the last letter is *n,* I know that's right." She looks up at the chalkboard again. "Oh, that's a *w,* not a *u.* Those letters look alike. *W.* Wood is brown and starts with *w,* and *brown* has a *w* in it." Hanley crosses out her misspelled word and writes the word correctly this time. "That's it."

"Hanley, what is the word?"

"*Brown.*"

"Can you spell *brown?*"

"*B-r-o-w-n. Brown.*"

"Good work, Hanley. See how easy it is if you just look at the word. Look at it carefully and get a good picture of it in your mind."

Ms. Cullen points to the third word on the list and begins to discuss the shape of the word. During the entire lesson, Cy, a kinesthetic learner, has been busy looking for his pencil— moving books around and rubbing his hands over a pile of paper to see if he can feel it. He pushes his feet around under the desk to see if he can kick the pencil out into plain sight. As he becomes aware that attention is on him, his workbook falls to the floor.

Cy knows he was not paying attention. Ms. Cullen sees this, and says, "Why don't you come up to the board, Cy. Take this chalk and trace over the letters that make up this word." Cy walks to the front of the room and takes the chalk from Ms. Cullen.

The word on the board is *contest.* Cy begins tracing the letters while Ms. Cullen describes the word. Cy manages to trace over the word four times by the time Ms. Cullen has described it to the class. The teacher tells the class what the word is, and asks if anyone knows what it means. Before any of the other children can answer, Cy says, "It's like a race. You try to win against other people. Yesterday Charles and I had a contest to see who could swing the highest." Cy has walked over to Charles' desk and is standing beside it. It almost seems as if Cy is ready to start the contest again.

**Eager to participate, the kinesthetic learner would rather be moving about than in his seat.**

"Very good, Cy. I know you like contests. Why don't you go back to your seat and write the word." The child returns to his seat, picks up his pencil, and begins to write the word. At first, his letters are very large, almost the same size they were on the chalkboard. Cy has simply used the same muscle movements he did at the board. Ms. Cullen notices this and asks him to make his word smaller. Cy does this, eventually writing the word between the right lines. He walks up to Ms. Cullen to show her his work. She compliments him and sends him back to his seat.

She turns to us and says, "Cy sometimes spends more time in the aisles than in his chair."

Three children, three ways of learning. Kit learned how to spell the words because she could transfer the teacher's visual clues into her auditory strength by repeating the letters and sounds to herself. Hanley easily learned the spelling words because the lesson was taught through her own modality strength. Cy would have missed the lesson completely had the teacher presented the words only through visual or auditory means, since Cy does not yet know how to transfer auditory and visual cues into his kinesthetic strength. Ms. Cullen knew this, and by calling Cy to the board and allowing him to trace the letters, she presented the lesson to the boy in a way he can understand.

The adaptations Ms. Cullen made to the lesson were not difficult. They were based on her understanding of modality and her experience. She did not attempt to ignore her own preferred way of learning, nor did she force her method on her students. She began the lesson in the manner in which she was most confident and comfortable, and adapted it as she went along. By any criteria, Ms. Cullen is a good teacher.

## Modality-Based Instructional Materials

The teacher who understands modality-based instruction can adapt any material to utilize children's modality strengths. But educational publishers are beginning to respond to the use of modality-based instruction by structuring books and providing added strategies for visual, auditory, and kinesthetic learners. This is not a radical change, rather it is a refinement in our awareness of children and how they can learn from the printed materials they use every day.

A good example of modality-based material is a set of three alphabet charts produced by one publisher for basic reading instruction. Each chart uses words that call on visual, auditory, or kinesthetic strengths. These charts are part of reading skill kits that provide activities for the three learning styles from readiness through fourth grade. A teacher can select the appropriate strategy when working with a child on a skill such as initial consonant sounds. A visual child can develop a strong

**In these modality-specific cards, alphabet letters are presented in ways that appeal to visual, auditory, and kinesthetic learners.**

image of a word with a specific beginning sound; an auditory child can use the sound of the word; and a kinesthetic child can actually do the word while saying or listening for the sound.

## When You Visit the School

Visit your child's school. Look around and see what the classroom environment is like. You should not try to identify the teacher's modality strength from such brief information, but the classroom will tell you what kinds of things are available to your child in the course of the day. If there is something you know your child responds to and you don't see it, you might talk to the teacher about your understanding of your child and how he or she learns best. It is quite possible that there is a special resource room for listening to tapes and an art room for art supplies and lessons. Schools will have different space limitations and arrangements which may determine that many activities take place in one classroom or in different rooms throughout the building.

Do not expect that the school, the classroom, or the teacher will be the same as those you had when you were learning. The years you remember as your best learning times probably resulted from teachers who provided you with strategies in your modality strength. And the years that will be your child's best will result from strategies that match his or her strength. What worked for you may not be what works for your child. Do not be critical of a learning environment or a teacher until you have seen what works for the students in that class and how the teacher handles their different modality strengths.

When you go to observe a class, be careful not to interject yourself into the situation. Your goal is to see how your child works in the classroom, to support your observations made at home concerning your child's modality strength. Before you go, make a list of the things you are going to look for. If you are kinesthetic, keep your visit brief so you do not disrupt a lesson with your own movement. If you are visual, do not let a cluttered room distract you from observing the interaction that takes place between teacher and child. This will be a more honest indication of successful teaching and learning. If you are strongly auditory, remember just to *listen,* and hold your questions for the teacher until a later time. The parent-teacher conference is when the teacher can give you her full attention.

**Working with the teacher, you can help your child use his modality strength to learn effectively.**

Once you have attended a class, you can use your observations to help you work with your child and the teacher to achieve the most effective learning. You can help your child understand what happens in the classroom, how his or her own learning strengths can be used when faced with different materials and concepts. If there is a problem, be careful not to take sides. In many cases it is neither the teacher nor the child who is right or wrong. It is a question of how to do things differently.

The most important step to take when there is a problem is to define a single issue, not a multitude of symptoms. Clarify what the teacher thinks the problem is, what the child thinks the problem is, what you think the problem is. As you think about what is causing the problem, keep your child's strength in mind. The problem may well stem from occasions when she is asked to perform in her weakest area or when something is inhibiting her learning strength.

Minimizing the potential for trouble can help in some problem situations. If a kinesthetic child has a big, long, round pencil, a stack of books on her desk, and more paper than she needs, you can be sure the pencil will roll onto the floor, the books will be knocked off with a bang, and the paper will end up flying. When the teacher makes sure she has a smaller pencil with edges or a clip to stop it, a clear desk, and only the supplies she needs, both the child and the teacher will have an easier time.

## What To Do When Your Child Needs Help

Most children will go through their school years with expected ups and downs but no long-term problems. More than ever before, schools are able to cope with children's differences, whether related to development, learning disabilities, or giftedness. But what happens if your child does have real difficulty, if he just isn't learning as he should?

The first step is to talk with your child's teacher. For any conferences relating to your child it is most important for both parents to attend if at all possible. The insights from each parent concerning the child will be valuable to the teacher, and both parents will understand the problem and the approach to be taken toward correcting it.

There are several questions you can ask yourself after defining the real problem:

*What does my child do well?*
List all the things you can think of that your child excels in, or likes to do. Don't overlook answers that seem merely

humorous. The stock reply that a child's favorite subject is recess may be a clue to his strength. Does he like going to school? Does he like to do well? Does he like the teacher and the other children? Is he neat? Talkative? Active? Do not worry about what he's having trouble in. Find out all the positive elements, put them all together, and work from there.

*How does my child accomplish tasks in his positive areas?*
It is possible to structure studying in such a way that your child can do the things the way he likes when he has to work in his trouble areas. If he is kinesthetic, keep study periods brief. If you approach a task with the goal of working until everything is finished (especially when it's forty problems and two hours of effort) you have doomed the kinesthetic child to failure before you start. Let him do a few problems as soon as he gets home, then he can go out to play for a time. Do a few more problems before dinner, a few after dinner, a few later in the evening. By interspersing breaks between study periods you are not demanding more than his attention can give. Work with the teacher to find appropriate ways to adapt study times to match your child's way of doing things.

*How can we, as parents, and the school be mutually supportive?*
You and the teacher both want your child to succeed. No one should be put in the position of being the adversary, neither you or your child against the teacher, nor she against you. The teacher must think of the whole class much of the time. She simply cannot manage a whole curriculum in individual ways. She must understand that you are vitally interested in doing something to help your child and that you can work together to find ways of supporting what she is doing. Your child's success in school depends on the confidence you and the teacher share.

   If your efforts—together with the teacher's—are not successful, discuss what to do next. It is always wise to consult with your child's pediatrician to make sure there are no physical problems that have gone undiagnosed previously. There may be a hearing problem or a visual deficiency affecting your child's achievement. Be sure to follow up such a visit by sharing your information with the teacher.

If no physical problems are found, ask the teacher what diagnostic resources are available in the school system. Many schools have psychologists, counselors, and/or remedial specialists who can offer their special knowledge. You might ask to meet with the teacher and the principal together to discuss the problem. The principal is there to help both teacher and parent and is often able to look at a problem more objectively than those closest to it.

The different perspectives brought by professionals to a difficult case may in fact be the key to solving the problem. In a team approach, team members will bring different modality strengths to bear. When projecting their learning strengths they may find the key to helping a child with a similar strength. With your help, the teacher, counselor, psychologist, or remedial specialist can develop an educational plan for your child that recognizes his or her learning strengths. When a child begins to experience success in his own abilities and learns how he learns best, then he will continue to grow according to his own potential.

Modality-based education is not the ultimate solution to every problem faced by teachers and parents today. But it is one approach that is effective for many learners who have known little success in school. It is a tool for diagnosing problems and a plan for realizing achievement for gifted, average, and slow learners. To all children it brings self-awareness and self-confidence in their unique talents and abilities, and it encourages them to use their strengths in any direction they may go.

*Chapter 11*

# Helping Your Child Capitalize on Learning Strengths

The key to helping children achieve all that they can be is *learning to learn*. Beginning before the child enters school, and continuing through the academic years as knowledge is acquired, knowing how one learns best ensures success. When your child knows how he or she learns, the strategy for approaching each new challenge in life will already be established.

I once asked a little boy if he liked reading and he gave the most sensible answer in the world, "I would if I knew how." We all like to do what we know how to do well. If children fail in the beginning stages of learning, they develop negative attitudes and consequently learn not to enjoy the process of learning. Before the first days of school, our task as parents is to help children acquire positive attitudes toward learning. They can best acquire these positive attitudes if their initial experiences in learning are successful. If the child is working in his area of strength, the chance for his success is greatly enhanced.

As adults we have all learned, often by blind trial and error, the areas in which we can be successful as well as those areas in which success is less likely. Instead of devoting our time to our weak areas, we select jobs that allow us to function in our area of strength, select friends who appreciate the kinds of skills we have, compete in those activities in which we have success, and conversely avoid our areas of weakness. Tragically, our approach to children's learning has been just the reverse. We have tended to find what the child could not do well and to concentrate on strengthening his weaknesses. A better strategy, which results in a happier and more successful child, is to find the child's area of strength. We can then work through that strength to provide him success both in his strong areas and in those areas which are more difficult.

**Working through children's strengths builds their confidence, ensures success, and can be fun, too!**

In your own family, understanding how each person perceives the world—through watching, talking, or doing—will make a big difference in developing strong communication channels. Learning to apply this knowledge to other relationships will make your child a more understanding adult. Learning to learn will make your child a more astute observer, a more perceptive listener, or a more constructive doer.

## Learning to Learn

We have explored the ways each person learns best and suggested ways to enhance learning strengths. Here are six rules to help you, as a parent, to be your child's first and best teacher, and to help her capitalize on her learning strength.

1. *Be aware of how your child learns best — kinesthetically, visually, auditorily, or a combination.*

Your own observations and the appropriate "Key to Your Child's Learning Strength" found in Chapter 3 will show you *how* your child learns.

2. *Be aware of how you learn best.*

Remember that your learning strength may be very different from your child's. Teach her, if you can, the way she learns best, not the way you do.

3. *Provide your child with opportunities for success in his or her modality.*

The toys, activities, and play you provide will help your child develop her learning strength and become more aware of how she learns best.

4. *Discipline and reward your child according to how he or she learns best.*

By matching communication styles to your child's needs, you will be providing the input he receives best. Your communication will be effective, and you and your child can develop a successful relationship.

5. *Always teach to your child's strengths rather than to weaknesses.*

Discuss with your child's teacher your observations of how he learns. Ask how you can reinforce the teaching of basic skills with learning activities in your home.

Your child will grow into a self-confident adult if he knows his strengths and how to use them rather than being constantly frustrated by his weaknesses. Working on improving a weakness might mean a slight or temporary difference, but enhancing a strength will give him a tool he can use with confidence all his life.

6. *Help your child apply basic modality strategies to master more complex skills and concepts.*

The study techniques that work best in learning basic skills—reading, spelling, arithmetic, and handwriting—will be used successfully in any new situation or challenge. This, of course, is what learning to learn means. It is not always easy to adjust the way in which we are taught to how we learn best, but the student who can do it will succeed.

## Which Is the Most Effective Learning Modality?

There is an unfortunate tendency on the part of all of us to think that there is some way other than the one we use that is more effective, or that our own style is the right one for everyone else. Once when I was speaking to a group of adults, during the question-and-answer session, one lady asked, "What modality is the best one to have?" Meaning to be humorous, and being a

**The best modality for every child is the one that he or she already has.**

person with a very strong visual mode, I promptly replied, "Visual." I assumed the lady would understand what I meant, but she missed my point and began to write down my response. In great distress I stopped her and explained, "Of course, the best modality to have is precisely the one that you do have."

To the extent that we learn to use our modality strengths, we can then function at the best possible level. To assume that any one modality is somehow "better" than the other or that a person is put in a position of disadvantage because he has one

*Growing Up Learning*

modality over another is completely erroneous. In some situations it is true that persons with certain modalities have more difficulty adapting than others, but it does not mean that one modality is better than another.

Kinesthetic children, for example, have more difficulty adjusting to the confinement of the classroom than do visual and auditory children. Even though there are as many kinesthetic girls as there are boys—about 15 percent of the total population—apparently girls are better able to adjust. This is the reason why so many more kinesthetic boys encounter learning difficulties in the elementary grades. In those school subjects that require extensive outside reading, visual students are favored. In purely lecture courses and music, auditory children are favored. In lab courses and physical education, kinesthetic students seem to be favored.

As adults, individuals' modalities tend to be a major factor in their career selection. Kinesthetic individuals, for instance, are attracted to those types of jobs that allow them to be doers. They tend to avoid the behind-the-desk type of activity, often favored by visual learners, and may very well be surgeons, dentists, mechanics, and other active professionals. Kinesthetic people who go into teaching are often found in coaching positions or in kindergarten, where so much learning is still hands-on. Auditory individuals tend to be attracted to sales positions, law, and other tasks requiring auditory input and interaction with other people. Visual people attend to detail more and make better accountants, teachers of certain subjects, and computer programmers.

## Children Doing Their Best

In your family relationships, matches and mismatches of different strengths may be the source of some difficulty. Simply being aware of each person's dominant modality is the first step to overcoming many problems. Whenever possible, ask each child (and your spouse!) to do what he or she does best. One kinesthetic mother was telling me that she knew she could rely on her visual son as a resource for finding and keeping track of all sorts of things. She was aware that she tended to put things down around the house wherever she happened to be. When she needed something later, like her car keys, she could never find them. They were never in the same place twice. But she had discovered that her son Mark always seemed to notice things and could recall with no trouble where he had last seen them. Not only that, her son always knew where everyone else was around the house. She had two other boys, and Mark was an enormous help when she needed to check on someone's whereabouts. This mother had discovered one child's strength and the knowledge helped them both. It was very rewarding for Mark to be able to help in this way and it made him feel good about himself.

When you have more than one child and each one has a different learning style, you will find yourself both as a mediator smoothing out recurrent clashes and as an observer to happy play of complementing styles. Your children will drive each other crazy as well as enjoy each other's various interests, all for the same reasons. Kinesthetic children will add energy to

**When children have different learning styles, they can often help each other by combining their talents.**

any occasion, for better or for worse. They may play too roughly sometimes and always win, but they defend siblings when needed and try to help in any physical endeavor. Auditory children may make too much noise when others need quiet, but they are also the ones to make up silly songs or put on the radio to liven the day and make everyone laugh. Visual children might "borrow" something of someone else's (just to *look* at it!), but they are also the ones who will draw a picture or write a special message for someone. When opportunities arise, help your children to see each other's strengths. When one child needs to concentrate, studying for a test or finishing a difficult project, respect her enough to meet her needs whether for quiet, for a sounding board, or for a space to work. Other times, let your children learn how they can help and enrich each other by combining their talents and appreciating individual differences rather than criticizing.

On occasion, a difference between parent and child or between two children will come down to what is most important to those involved. The answer will be determined by the particular situation and the feelings of the family members. Let us say the father in a family is highly visual and extremely organized. He values neatness and organization throughout his home. His nine-year-old daughter is not visual and her room reflects her style—things are not put away, posters hang askew on the walls, and her desk is a jumble of stuff. The father may accept keeping the door to his daughter's room closed so that he is not bothered by seeing the mess, and she is given responsibility for her own area. Or the father may make an agreement with his daughter—asking that his priority for neatness be met for which he will give something in return. For example, if she cleans the room, he will ride bikes with her (or whatever activity she chooses as a reward).

Such an agreement may hold its own potential problems. In the example above, the father and daughter should agree on a sequence of standards to be met. It is unlikely that she will clean her room immaculately the very first time; if she is rewarded for *improvement* each time she cleans her room, instead of perfection, the agreement is more likely to succeed. As family members contend with problems, it is important that they keep their expectations realistic when dealing with each other. The key to successful compromises is to allow each person input about what influences him or her. And when trying a new solution to an old problem, gentle reminders may be helpful since old habits are hard to change.

You know your family better than anyone. You know how each member works best. It is up to you to use what will work for your own child and to expand on these strategies in whatever ways your child needs.

By knowing more of how you learn and how your child learns, you can take these insights and help your child be an enthusiastic and effective learner all through his life. Developing one's full potential is achieved by growing up learning.

# Selected
# Readings

Bank Street College. *The Pleasure of Their Company.* Radnor, Pennsylvania: Chilton Book Co., 1981.

Barbe, Walter B. and Swassing, Raymond H. *Teaching Through Modality Strengths: Concepts and Practices.* Columbus, Ohio: Zaner-Bloser, Inc., 1979.

Behrmann, Polly and Millman, Joan. *Excel: Experience for Children in Learning.* Cambridge, Massachusetts: Educators Publishing Service, 1968.

Burie, Audrey Ann and Heltshe, Mary Ann. *Reading with a Smile.* Washington, D.C.: Acropolis Books, 1975.

Cleveland, Bernard F. *Master Teaching Techniques.* Stone Mountain Georgia: The Connecting Link Press, 1984.

Constructive Playthings Catalogue. Grandview, Missouri: U.S. Toy Co., 1985-1986.

Dunn, Rita. "How Should Students Do Their Homework? Research vs. Opinion," *Early Years.* Darien, Connecticut: Allen Raymond, Inc. (December, 1984): 43-45.

Dunn, Rita and Dunn, Kenneth. "What Is Your Child's Learning Style?" *The Newsletter of Parenting.* Columbus, Ohio: Highlights for Children 3, 1 (January, 1980): 4-5, 8.

Dunn, Rita and Dunn, Kenneth. *Teaching Students Through Their Individual Learning Styles.* Reston, Virginia: Reston Publishing Co., 1978.

Gregorc, Anthony. "Learning Style/Brain Research: Harbinger of an Emerging Psychology." *Student Learning Styles and Brain Behavior.* Reston, Virginia: National Association of Secondary School Principals, 1982.

Keefe, James W., ed. *Student Learning Styles and Brain Behavior.* Reston, Virginia: National Association of Secondary School Principals, 1982.

Lamme, Linda Leonard. *Growing Up Reading.* Washington, D.C.: Acropolis Books, 1985.

Lamme, Linda Leonard. *Growing Up Writing.* Washington, D.C.: Acropolis Books, 1984.

Maxwell, Margaret John. *Listening Games for Elementary Grades.* Washington, D.C.: Acropolis Books, 1981.

Pai, Hang Y. *Complete Book of Chisanbop: Original Finger Calculation Method.* Edited by John Leonard. New York: Van Nostrand Reinhold, 1981.

Pearson, C. "Do you know how to Chisanbop?" *Learning,* 1978, 7, 134-138.

Touw, Kathleen. *Parent Tricks of the Trade.* Washington, D.C.: Acropolis Books, 1983.

Trelease, Jim. *The Read-Aloud Handbook.* New York: Penguin Books, 1982.

# Index

Abacus, 64
Action rhymes, 144-146
Adapting modality strengths, 197
Alphabet
  charts, 187-188
  evolution of, 20-21
Arithmetic
  auditory strategies, 80-81
  kinesthetic strategies, 64-65
  visual strategies, 94-95
Auditory child
  communication with, 70, 71, 76
  description of, 69-73
  discipline of, 75-76
  in class, 72, 78, 183-184
  in testing situation, 24
  providing for, 73-74
  reading, 78-80
  rewards for, 76-77
  study habits, 82
Auditory modality
  characteristics of, 25-26
  definition of, 16
  percentage of population, 25
  teaching methods, 21
Auditory parent, 33, 35-36
  communication with, 27, 35-36, 37
  environment, 33
Auditory strategies
  arithmetic, 80-81
  handwriting, 80
  reading, 78-80
  spelling, 81-82
Auditory teacher
  classroom environment, 180-181
Auditory/kinesthetic child, 101-102

Barbe Modality Checklist
  interpreting results, 32, 46-47
  parents, 30-31

ages 0-4, 40-41
ages 5-8, 42-43
ages 9 and over, 44-45
Behavior modification chart, 89
Books
  appeal to each modality, 164-165
  five to eight-year-olds, 169-173
  nine-year-olds and above, 173-178
  preschoolers, 165-169

Careers, 102, 197
Chalkboard writing, 54, 61, 63, 87, 182
Child-parent relationship, 39, 57, 77, 90
Chisanbop, 65
Counselors, 192
Crafts, 160-163
Cuisenaire rods, 64

Dictating, 79
Discipline
  and the auditory child, 75-76
  and the kinesthetic child, 56
  and the visual child, 88
Dominant modality, 16
Dr. Seuss, 78, 164, 168

Edmunds Scientific Co., 73
Eye-hand coordination, 104

Finger plays, 144-146
Finger pointing, 61
Flash cards, 64, 95, 183
Frostig, Marianne, 22

Games, 111-131
  adapting to modality strength, 109-110
Greeks, ancient, 20-21

Handwriting
  auditory strategies, 80
  kinesthetic strategies, 63-64
  visual strategies, 93-94
Hyperactivity, 10, 54

Incas, 21

Kinesthetic child
  description of, 51-56
  discipline of, 56
  communication with, 53
  in class, 58-59, 185-186
  in testing situation, 24
  involved in reading, 59-63
  providing for, 54, 57-58
  rewards for, 56-57
  study habits, 66-68
Kinesthetic modality
  characteristics of, 25-26
  definition of, 16
  percentage of population, 25
  teaching methods, 21
Kinesthetic parent, 197-198
  communication with, 27, 36
  environment, 33
Kinesthetic strategies
  arithmetic, 64-65
  handwriting, 63-64
  reading, 59-62
  spelling, 65-66
Kinesthetic teacher
  classroom environment, 181-182

Large muscle, small muscle
  movements, 54, 60, 65, 186
Learning strength (see Modality,
  Auditory, Kinesthetic, Visual;
  see also Modality, dominant)
  identifying, 24
Left-to-right progression, 60-61,
  135-136
Listening games, 74, 79, 113, 117,
  121, 141, 142

Manuscript basic strokes, 94
Matching activities, 137-140
Mixed modality, 17
  description of, 98-100
  examples of, 47, 97-99

percentage of population, 24-25
Modality (see also Auditory,
  Kinesthetic, Visual)
  changes in relative strength, 48
  characteristics (table), 25-26
  differences within family, 36-37,
    38, 49, 198-200
  dominant, 16
  examples of, 47
  influenced by sex, handedness,
    or race, 48
  integration of, 32
  interference, 68, 77
  mixed, 32 (see also Mixed
    modality)
  secondary, 16
  weaknesses, 15, 18, 22-23, 68,
    77, 93
Modality-based education, 179,
  192
  definition of, 23
  history of, 20-23
Modality-based instructional
  materials, 187-188
Modality-specific activities (table),
  50
Modality-specific toys (table), 50
Montessori, Maria, 21-22
Motivation, 62, 157
Multi-sensory instruction, 23
Music, 53, 71

Newspaper writing, 63
Note taking, 36, 95-96

Paper position, manuscript, 64
Parent
  working with teacher, 188-192
Parties
  Circus party, 122-125
  Snowman party, 125-127
  Topsy-turvy party, 128-131
Pediatrician, 191
Pencil position, 64
Perception, 16
Phonetic approach to spelling, 81
Phonetic teaching methods, 21
Phonics approach to reading, 79,
  92-93

Point of intervention, 59, 78, 91
Psychologist, 192

Quipu, 21

Reading
  auditory strategies, 78-80
  book list, 164-178
  comprehension, 78-79, 147
  kinesthetic strategies, 59-62
  phonetic approach, 105
  readiness activities, 135-147
  remedial specialists, 192
  sight word approach, 105, 185
  visual strategies, 91-93
Rewards
  for auditory child, 76-77
  for kinesthetic child, 56-57
  for visual child, 88-89
Rhyming activities, 141-146
Rogers, Will, 18
Romans, ancient, 21

Secondary modality, 16
Spelling
  auditory strategies, 81-82
  kinesthetic strategies, 65-66
  visual strategies, 95
Swassing-Barbe Modality Index,
    48

Tape recorder and tapes, 73,
    180-181
Teacher
  working with parent, 188-192
  and student modalities, 106
Thinking activities, 147-156
Toys, 50, 132-134
  for auditory child, 73-74
  for kinesthetic child, 54-55

for visual child, 87-88
Tracing, 186
Tricks and teasers, 157-159

Visual/auditory child, 100-101
Visual/auditory/kinesthetic child,
    104-107
Visual child
  communication with, 85, 86, 90
  description of, 83-87
  difficulty with phonics, 92-93
  discipline of, 88
  in class, 185
  in testing situation, 24
  providing for, 87-88
  reading, 91-93
  rewards for, 88-89
  study habits, 95-96
Visual/kinesthetic child, 103-104
Visual modality
  characteristics of, 25-26
  definition of, 16
  percentage of population, 24
  teaching methods, 21
  teaching methods, preference for,
    21, 22
Visual parent, 32, 34-35
  communication with, 27, 34-35
  environment, 32
Visual strategies
  arithmetic, 94-95
  handwriting, 93-94
  reading, 91-93
  spelling, 95
Visual teacher
  classroom environment, 182-183
  instructional strategy, 183-187

Word configuration, 183-184, 185

Sharing with Your Children the Joys of Good Writing
Linda Leonard Lamme, Ph.D.
Foreword by Walter B. Barbe, Ph.D., Editor-in-Chief, Highlights for Children

## Highlights for Children
## Growing Up Writing

Sharing with Your Children
The Joys of Good Writing

*by Linda Leonard Lamme, Ph.D.*
*foreword by Walter B. Barbe, Ph.D.*
*Editor-in-Chief, Highlights for Children*

Children whose parents involve them actively with
writing experiences from early childhood are far better
equipped for school. In fact, home writing experiences far
outweigh school experiences in helping children become
lifelong writers. The parent's role is critical, especially in
the formative years.

*Growing Up Writing* was written by Dr. Linda Lamme,
Professor of Elementary and Early Childhood Education at
the University of Florida, in cooperation with the respected
children's magazine, *Highlights for Children*. Dr. Lamme's
and *Highlights'* goal in this book is to offer parents insight
into how their children develop as writers and to give them
ideas for encouraging children to write.

Topics include... • When to Begin • Early Scribbling
• How Parents Can Help • From Scribblings to Writing
• Tools • Providing Time for Writing • Word Awareness

ISBN 87491-760-3/$8.95 quality paper/Parenting
250 pages, 6 × 9, illustrations

Sharing with Your Children the Joys of Reading
Linda Leonard Lamme, Ph.D.
Foreword by Walter B. Barbe, Ph.D. Editor-in-Chief, Highlights for Children

## Highlights for Children
## Growing Up Reading
Sharing with Your Children
the Joys of Reading

*by Linda Leonard Lamme, Ph.D.*
*foreword by Walter B. Barbe, Ph.D.*
*Editor-in-Chief, Highlights for Children*

**NOW, reading can become a fun family activity!**

*Growing Up Reading* shares many ideas and activities
with parents for encouraging a love of reading in their
children from the very beginning. Parents don't need to
worry about "teaching" their children to read. They will
learn naturally if they are surrounded by adults who enjoy
reading, who read to them and who are responsive to their
curiosity.

Early Childhood Professor Linda Lamme worked with
*Highlights for Children* to make reading an enjoyable,
natural family activity because they believe that the home
is the first and most important learning environment that a
child will ever have.

*Growing Up Reading* is a companion volume to *Growing
Up Writing.* Together these two books give parents
hundreds of ideas and activities.

ISBN 87491-777-8/$8.95 quality paper/Parenting
224 pages, 6 × 9, illustrations, index
Publication date: April 1985
• National promotion in cooperation with *Highlights for Children*
  at parent and teacher conventions and workshops.

*About the Author*

Dr. Walter B. Barbe is Editor-in-Chief of HIGHLIGHTS FOR CHILDREN and Adjunct Professor at The Ohio State University. He is senior author of both the Zaner-Bloser handwriting and spelling series.

Dr. Barbe is one of the most respected educators in America today. For over three decades, his work as a teacher, professor, psychologist, and author has contributed to the understanding of how children learn. He has published over 250 professional articles and monographs and eight professional books for teachers. He is a fellow of the American Psychological Association, and is listed in *American Men in Science* and *Who's Who in America*.

Among the most significant trends in education today is the learning styles movement. Dr. Walter Barbe was a pioneer in this movement with his work on modality strengths and is the senior author of a professional book, a diagnostic test, a series of instructional materials, and a dozen articles and pamphlets that deal with modality.

Dr. Barbe's informative yet enjoyable style makes him much in demand as a consultant and speaker. In *Growing Up Learning* he brings to the reader knowledge and enthusiasm, and conveys his love for children and his deep respect for parents and teachers.